QUANTUM MIND

INVISIBLE CONNECTIONS

Explore the connections between neuroscience, cognitive psychology, and the power of attraction through quantum physics

By Marco Silvestri

Copyright © 2024 by Marco Silvestri
All rights reserved. No part of this book may be reproduced in any form without written permission from the publisher, except as permitted by Italian copyright law.

Sommario

INTRODUCTION 5

Chapter 1 7

Introduction to the Quantum Mind 7

Chapter 2 22

The Foundations of Quantum Physics 22

Chapter 3 38

Neuroscience of Perception and Consciousness 38

Chapter 4 55

Cognitive Psychology: Thoughts and Beliefs 55

Chapter 5 71

The Theory of Attraction and Quantum Connections 71

Chapter 6 86

The Entanglement of the Mind 86

Chapter 7 102

Superposition and Infinite Potential 102

Chapter 8 118

The Role of the Observer 118

Chapter 9 134

Neuroscience and Meditation 134

Chapter 10 150

Invisible Connections in Relationships 150
Chapter 11 168
Practical Applications of the Quantum Mind . 168
Chapter 12 184
The Future of the Quantum Mind 184

INTRODUCTION

Dear Reader,

Welcome to "Quantum Mind: Invisible Connections," a journey that will take you to the edge of science and the infinite. I am Marco Silvestri, and I have written this book for you, for anyone who has ever gazed at the starry sky and wondered how the vastness of the universe can resonate within us.

This book is the result of a personal journey of discovery and deep reflection on the most significant questions of existence. It is an invitation to explore together the wonders of the human mind and understand how the laws of quantum physics can influence our daily reality and well-being.

In these pages, I will guide you through the mysteries of consciousness, perception, and reality itself. I will show you how modern science and ancient wisdom intertwine, revealing a connective fabric that unites every aspect of life. "Quantum Mind" is not just a book of theories; it is a map that will help you navigate the deep waters of knowledge and self-awareness.

With clear and accessible language, I will accompany you on an exploration of neuroscience, cognitive psychology, and quantum physics, demonstrating how these seemingly distant disciplines are actually intertwined in a continuous dialogue that can enrich our understanding of the world.

I invite you to be inspired by the stories of those who have used quantum principles to transform their lives, to reflect on the power of the mind to influence reality, and to consider the ethical and spiritual implications of a quantum view of existence.

This book is a tribute to your curiosity and your desire for personal growth. It is a recognition of your ability to wonder and seek the truth. It acknowledges your role as both observer and creator of your reality. "Quantum Mind: Invisible Connections" is an invitation to challenge your beliefs, expand your awareness, and discover new possibilities for your life.

I wish you an enlightening and transformative journey, full of discoveries and insights. May this book be a source of inspiration and a starting point for a path of ever-deepening growth and understanding.

With affection and gratitude for your time and presence,

Marco Silvestri

Chapter 1

Introduction to the Quantum Mind

Definition of Quantum Mind and Overview of the Themes Covered in the Book

The quantum mind is a concept that combines advanced theories of quantum physics with neuroscience and cognitive psychology, offering a new perspective on how our brain perceives and interacts with reality. This concept arises from the need to understand the complex and seemingly inexplicable phenomena that influence our daily lives, from sudden insights to deep connections we feel with other people. The quantum mind is based on the idea that our consciousness is not limited by the physical boundaries of the brain, but can interact with the universe on a much more fundamental and interconnected level.

In this book, we will explore how principles of quantum physics, such as superposition and entanglement, can explain mental and emotional phenomena that traditional science struggles to comprehend. Quantum physics has revolutionized our understanding of the physical world, revealing that subatomic particles can exist in multiple states simultaneously and can influence each other at a distance, instantly. These concepts find surprising parallels in the way our mind works, suggesting that the reality we perceive is strongly influenced by our thoughts and intentions.

We will also examine how neuroscience has discovered that the human brain is extremely plastic and capable of adapting and changing in response to experiences. This implies that our thoughts and beliefs can physically alter our brain and, consequently, our perceived reality. Cognitive psychology, with its focus on the inner workings of the mind, offers us additional tools to understand how we process information and how we can change our mental patterns to improve our lives.

One of the main themes of the book will be the theory of attraction, which suggests that our thoughts and emotions have the power to attract experiences and circumstances into our lives. This principle, often discussed in self-help and spirituality, can find a scientific basis in the principles of quantum physics and neuroscience. We will explore how intention and focused attention can influence our environment in ways that seem magical but are, in fact, deeply rooted in science.

The book will be divided into three main sections: the first section will provide a solid theoretical foundation, introducing the fundamental principles of quantum physics, neuroscience, and cognitive psychology. The second section will explore the practical applications of these principles, showing how they can be used to improve various aspects of our lives, from interpersonal relationships to achieving our goals. Finally, the third section will look to the future, speculating on how these discoveries could transform our understanding of the mind and reality in the coming decades.

Through a combination of scientific theory, concrete examples, and practical advice, this book aims to guide the reader on a journey of discovery and transformation. The quantum mind is not just an abstract concept but a powerful lens through which we can see and interact with the world in new and more effective ways. By exploring the invisible connections that link our mind to the universe, we will discover how we can influence our reality and live a fuller and more meaningful life.

Brief History of Quantum Physics and Its Theoretical Implications

Quantum physics is one of the most fascinating and revolutionary areas of modern science. Its history began at the start of the 20th century when physicists started exploring phenomena that could not be explained by Newton's classical laws of physics. The starting point of this new scientific era can be traced back to the works of Max Planck and Albert Einstein, two of the greatest geniuses in the history of science.

In 1900, Max Planck introduced the concept of energy quantization to explain the problem of black body radiation. Planck proposed that energy was not continuous, as previously thought, but was emitted or absorbed in discrete quantities called "quanta." This revolutionary idea marked the birth of quantum theory and paved the way for a new understanding of the subatomic world.

A few years later, Albert Einstein extended Planck's ideas to explain the photoelectric effect, a phenomenon in which light striking a metallic surface can release electrons. Einstein proposed that light was composed of energy quanta called photons and that the energy of these photons was proportional to the light's frequency. This work earned him the Nobel Prize in Physics in 1921 and demonstrated that light possesses both wave-like and particle-like properties, a concept known as wave-particle duality.

In the 1920s, quantum theory was further developed by physicists like Niels Bohr, Werner Heisenberg, and Erwin Schrödinger. Niels Bohr proposed the quantum atomic model, in which electrons orbit the atomic nucleus in discrete energy levels. Werner Heisenberg formulated the uncertainty principle, which states that it is impossible to simultaneously and precisely know both the position and velocity of a particle. This principle suggests that the act of observing a particle affects its state.

Erwin Schrödinger, on the other hand, developed the wave equation, which mathematically describes the behavior of subatomic particles as probability waves. According to the Copenhagen interpretation of quantum mechanics, formulated by Bohr and Heisenberg, a subatomic particle does not have a definite position or state until it is observed. Before observation, it exists in a superposition of possible states, each with a certain probability.

Another key concept in quantum physics is entanglement, introduced by Schrödinger in 1935. When two particles become entangled, their properties remain connected regardless of the distance between them. This phenomenon was described by Einstein, Podolsky, and Rosen (EPR) in their famous paradox, which sought to demonstrate the incompleteness of quantum mechanics. However, subsequent experiments have confirmed the reality of entanglement, challenging our intuitive understanding of spatial separation.

Quantum physics has profound and often counterintuitive implications that have pushed the limits of our understanding of reality. For example, the idea that reality can be influenced by observation has led to new philosophical and scientific discussions about the nature of consciousness and reality itself. Moreover, quantum mechanics underpins many modern technologies, such as semiconductors, lasers, and quantum cryptography.

In our journey through the concept of the quantum mind, it is essential to understand these foundations of quantum physics. The principles of superposition, entanglement, and the role of the observer not only explain subatomic phenomena but also offer a new perspective on how our mind might interact with the universe. This history of quantum physics, though complex and often paradoxical, prepares us to explore the deep and invisible connections that bind our consciousness to the very fabric of reality.

Introduction to Neuroscience and Cognitive Psychology

Neuroscience and cognitive psychology are two disciplines that, while having distinct approaches and methods, are deeply intertwined in exploring the human mind. These sciences help us understand not only how our brain functions but also how our thoughts, emotions, and behaviors are shaped by brain processes.

Neuroscience studies the nervous system, with particular focus on the structure and function of the brain. Thanks to technological advancements in recent decades, such as functional magnetic resonance imaging (fMRI) and electroencephalography (EEG), scientists can observe the brain in action and see how different areas are activated during specific mental and behavioral tasks. These tools have allowed precise mapping of the brain areas responsible for functions such as language, memory, sensory perception, and motor control.

One of the most fascinating discoveries in neuroscience is brain plasticity, which refers to the brain's ability to reorganize and adapt in response to experiences. This means that our brain is dynamic and constantly evolving, capable of forming new neural connections and modifying existing ones. Brain plasticity underlies learning and memory, allowing us to acquire new skills and adapt to environmental and personal changes.

Cognitive psychology, on the other hand, focuses on internal mental processes such as perception, attention, memory, thinking, and language. Cognitive psychologists study how people process information, make decisions, and solve problems. This discipline emerged in the 1950s and 1960s as a reaction to behaviorism, which focused only on observable behavior and neglected internal mental processes.

One of the key concepts in cognitive psychology is the information processor model, which likens the human mind to a computer. According to this model, the brain receives sensory information, processes it through various stages, and produces behavioral responses. This approach has led to the development of detailed theories and models on how the mind works, such as the Atkinson and Shiffrin memory model, which divides memory into three main components: sensory memory, short-term memory, and long-term memory.

Neuroscience and cognitive psychology come together to offer a comprehensive view of the human mind. While neuroscience provides a biological and physiological understanding of the brain, cognitive psychology helps us understand how these processes translate into complex mental experiences and behaviors. For example, neuroimaging studies have revealed that specific brain areas are activated during memory tasks, confirming cognitive theories about the division of memory into different stages and systems.

These disciplines also have significant practical applications. Neuroscience has contributed to the development of treatments for neurological and psychiatric disorders, such as Parkinson's disease, depression, and anxiety, through the use of drugs, behavioral therapies, and neuromodulatory interventions. Cognitive psychology, on its part, has influenced education by improving teaching and learning methods and has impacted psychotherapy by providing techniques to modify dysfunctional thoughts and enhance mental well-being.

In this book, the intersection of neuroscience, cognitive psychology, and quantum physics will allow us to explore how the human mind interacts with the world in ways that challenge traditional understanding. Understanding these fields will provide us with the tools to investigate the invisible connections that bind our consciousness to reality, opening new possibilities for personal change and growth. The synergy between these disciplines will guide us toward a deeper understanding of ourselves and our place in the universe.

The Theory of Attraction: Principles and Scientific Foundations

The theory of attraction is a fascinating and controversial concept that has gained popularity through self-help books, films, and seminars. Essentially, this theory suggests that our thoughts, emotions, and intentions can directly influence our experiences and the reality around us. The fundamental principle is that "like attracts like": positive thoughts attract positive experiences, while negative thoughts attract negative ones.

At the core of the theory of attraction is the idea that everything in the universe, including thoughts, is composed of energy. Our thoughts emit a vibrational frequency that interacts with the vibrational frequencies of the surrounding environment, attracting events, people, and circumstances that resonate at the same frequency. This concept is closely related to the law of resonance, which states that similar vibrations attract each other.

Quantum physics offers a possible theoretical framework to explain how the theory of attraction might work. As discussed in previous chapters, quantum physics has revealed that subatomic particles can exist in multiple states simultaneously and that the observer affects the behavior of these particles. This suggests that our consciousness and thoughts might play a role in shaping reality.

A key experiment often cited in relation to the theory of attraction is the double-slit experiment. This experiment demonstrates that particles of light (photons) behave both as waves and particles, depending on the presence of an observer. When not observed, the photons pass through both slits simultaneously, creating an interference pattern. However, when a measure is taken to observe through which slit the photons pass, they behave as particles, passing through only one slit. This phenomenon highlights the crucial role of observation in determining reality.

Neuroscience provides further insights into how our thoughts can influence our reality. Brain plasticity, the brain's ability to change and adapt in response to experiences, implies that our thoughts and intentions can actually change the structure and function of our brain. For example, meditation and positive visualization have been shown to increase the density of gray matter in areas of the brain associated with emotion regulation and awareness.

Cognitive psychology contributes to understanding the theory of attraction through the concept of self-fulfilling prophecies. When we firmly believe in something, our actions and behaviors tend to create the conditions for that belief to become reality. If we believe we will succeed, we are more likely to seize opportunities, act with confidence, and persevere in the face of difficulties, thereby increasing the chances of success.

Critics of the theory of attraction argue that it can promote magical thinking and fails to account for the complex social, economic, and cultural dynamics that influence a person's life. However, even critics recognize the importance of maintaining a positive and proactive attitude in everyday life.

In this book, we will explore how the theory of attraction can be applied practically and consciously, using the knowledge of quantum physics, neuroscience, and cognitive psychology. We will delve into techniques of visualization, meditation, and intention setting to help the reader harness the power of their thoughts to create a more desirable reality. We will also examine case studies and personal experiences to illustrate how these principles can operate in real life, offering a balanced guide that combines science and practice to understand and apply the theory of attraction.

Through this exploration, we hope to provide a deeper understanding of how our thoughts and intentions can influence the world around us and offer practical tools for living a fuller and more meaningful life.

Goals of the Book and How These Interdisciplinary Fields Interconnect

The goals of this book are ambitious and deeply transformative. We aim to provide the reader with an integrated understanding of how quantum physics, neuroscience, and cognitive psychology can connect to explain and enhance the human experience. Through an interdisciplinary lens, we will explore the invisible connections that permeate our existence and show how to use this knowledge to live a more conscious, fulfilling, and empowered life.

One of the main objectives is to demystify quantum physics and make it accessible and relevant to everyday life. Often considered an abstract and complex discipline, quantum physics can seem distant from our personal experience. However, its fundamental principles, such as superposition, entanglement, and the observer effect, have implications that deeply touch our reality. This book aims to explain these concepts clearly and comprehensively, linking them to phenomena that we can directly observe and experience.

In parallel, we will delve into neuroscience to understand how the brain and nervous system process information, forming the basis for our perception and awareness. Neuroscience offers us a detailed view of the inner workings of the mind, explaining how experiences shape the structure and function of the brain. By examining brain plasticity, we will show how we can consciously influence our brain through targeted practices, improving our ability to think critically, manage emotions, and achieve our goals.

Cognitive psychology, with its focus on internal mental processes, provides us with the tools to understand how we interpret and react to the world around us. We will explore how our thought patterns, beliefs, and expectations shape our personal reality. Through cognitive change techniques, we will demonstrate how we can transform limiting thoughts and beliefs into powerful resources for success and well-being.

A fundamental goal of the book is to show how these three fields interconnect to create a complete picture of the human mind and its capabilities. Quantum physics provides us with the theoretical basis to understand how consciousness can influence reality. Neuroscience offers biological evidence of how the brain can be shaped by experiences and intentions. Cognitive psychology gives us practical techniques to change our thought patterns and improve our daily lives.

This interdisciplinary approach not only enriches our theoretical understanding but also provides practical tools that we can apply in everyday life. Through exercises in visualization, meditation, and intention setting, we will show readers how they can harness the power of the mind to positively influence their reality. Each chapter will offer practical exercises and applicable strategies to put the discussed concepts into practice, making the book not only a source of knowledge but also a practical guide for personal transformation.

Additionally, we will examine real-life stories and case studies to illustrate how these principles can be successfully applied. These testimonials will provide inspiration and concreteness, demonstrating that the theories discussed are not just abstract ideas but powerful tools for real change.

In conclusion, the goal of this book is to provide readers with a profound and integrated understanding of how quantum physics, neuroscience, and cognitive psychology can work together to improve our lives. Through a combination of theory, practice, and inspiration, we hope to guide readers toward greater awareness and personal power, revealing the invisible connections that bind the mind to the universe and offering a roadmap to navigate the vast potential of our existence.

Chapter 2

The Foundations of Quantum Physics

The Concept of Superposition and Heisenberg's Uncertainty Principle

The concept of superposition and Heisenberg's uncertainty principle are two of the fundamental pillars of quantum physics, capable of disrupting our traditional understanding of reality. These concepts, though complex, are essential for exploring how the subatomic world functions in a completely different manner from the macroscopic world we are accustomed to.

Quantum superposition is one of the most fascinating and strange phenomena in physics. In simple terms, superposition indicates that a particle, such as an electron or a photon, can simultaneously exist in multiple states until it is observed. This means that a particle can be in different places at the same time or have different velocities simultaneously. It is only at the moment of measurement that the particle "chooses" a definite state. This behavior is mathematically described by the wave function, which represents the probability of finding the particle in a specific state.

To make this concept more tangible, consider the famous thought experiment of Schrödinger's cat. Imagine a cat locked in a box with a mechanism that has a 50% chance of killing it based on the decay of a radioactive particle. According to quantum physics, until we open the box to observe the state of the cat, it is simultaneously alive and dead. This superposition of states seems paradoxical but is a direct consequence of quantum laws.

Heisenberg's uncertainty principle, formulated by German physicist Werner Heisenberg in 1927, introduces another level of strangeness into the quantum world. This principle states that it is impossible to simultaneously and precisely know two complementary properties of a particle, such as its position and velocity (momentum). In other words, the more precisely we know the position of a particle, the less precisely we can know its velocity, and vice versa.

This principle is not due to limitations of our instrumentation but is an intrinsic property of nature. Heisenberg demonstrated that this uncertainty is a consequence of wave-particle duality and the wave-like behavior of matter. This has profound philosophical and scientific implications: reality, at the subatomic level, is not deterministic but probabilistic.

Superposition and the uncertainty principle are deeply connected. The wave function that describes a particle in superposition is closely related to the probability of finding the particle in a certain state when observed. The act of observation, which causes the wave function to collapse, is also the moment when the uncertainty principle manifests, limiting the precision with which we can simultaneously know the particle's properties.

These concepts have been confirmed by numerous experiments, such as the double-slit experiment, where particles like electrons create an interference pattern typical of waves when not observed but behave as individual particles when measured. This experiment highlights how observation directly influences particle behavior, emphasizing the importance of the observer's role in quantum physics.

Understanding superposition and the uncertainty principle leads us to a radically different view of reality from that proposed by classical physics. In this new paradigm, the world is not a collection of objects with defined properties but an intricate fabric of probabilities and possibilities that materialize only through interaction with the observer's consciousness. This has profound implications not only for physics but also for our understanding of the mind and reality, themes we will explore in detail in the subsequent chapters of this book.

Quantum Entanglement and Its Implications

Quantum entanglement is one of the most extraordinary and mysterious phenomena of modern physics, capable of challenging our intuition and revolutionizing the way we understand the universe. First described by Albert Einstein, Boris Podolsky, and Nathan Rosen in the famous EPR paradox in 1935, quantum entanglement refers to a phenomenon where two or more particles become so intimately linked that the state of one particle instantaneously depends on the state of the other, regardless of the distance separating them.

Imagine we have two entangled particles, A and B. If we measure the state of A, we will immediately know the state of B, even if the particles are light-years apart. This phenomenon seems to violate the principle of locality, which states that physical influences cannot propagate faster than the speed of light. For this reason, Einstein referred to entanglement as "spooky action at a distance," as it challenged his view of a local and realistic universe.

Quantum entanglement has significant theoretical and practical implications. One of its first experimental confirmations came from Alain Aspect's experiments in the 1980s, which convincingly demonstrated that entangled particles violate Bell's inequalities, confirming that entanglement is real and cannot be explained by local hidden variables. These results established that quantum physics accurately describes subatomic reality and that entangled particles are indeed non-locally correlated.

The practical implications of quantum entanglement are immense and are already revolutionizing various technologies. For example, entanglement is the foundation of quantum cryptography, a method for creating secure communications that is theoretically unbreakable. In a quantum cryptography system, two users can share a secret key generated by entangled particles. Any attempt to intercept the key would alter the state of the particles, making it immediately evident that security has been compromised.

Another emerging field that exploits entanglement is quantum computing. Quantum computers use qubits, which can exist in a superposition of states thanks to entanglement, allowing them to perform many operations simultaneously. This could lead to exponentially greater computing power compared to classical computers, revolutionizing fields such as the simulation of complex molecular systems, optimization, and solving advanced mathematical problems.

Perhaps the most fascinating implications of quantum entanglement lie in its ability to expand our understanding of reality. Entanglement suggests that the universe is inherently interconnected and that apparent separations are merely a facade of a deeper, unified reality. This concept resonates with various philosophical and spiritual traditions that have long maintained that everything is interconnected.

In the context of the quantum mind, entanglement offers a powerful metaphor for understanding how our minds might be connected on a fundamental level. If particles can be correlated over vast distances, it might be possible that our minds and consciousnesses are part of a larger network of invisible interconnections. This could explain phenomena such as telepathy, sudden insights, and the feeling of deep connection with others.

In this book, we will explore how quantum entanglement can be used as a model to understand mental and emotional connections between individuals. We will discuss studies and experiments suggesting the possibility of non-local interaction between human minds and how these discoveries can influence our perception of reality and our place in the universe.

Quantum entanglement is not just a theoretical curiosity but a gateway to a deeper understanding of universal interconnectedness. By continuing to explore this phenomenon, we may discover that we are all part of a quantum fabric that transcends space and time, united in ways we are only beginning to glimpse.

The Observer Effect and the Role of Consciousness in Quantum Physics

The observer effect is one of the most intriguing and debated concepts in quantum physics, raising profound questions about the nature of reality and the role of consciousness. This phenomenon suggests that the very act of observing or measuring a quantum particle can influence its state, altering the outcome of the experiment. In other words, the subatomic reality seems to be shaped by the intervention of the observer.

The famous double-slit experiment clearly illustrates the observer effect. In this experiment, when a particle, such as a photon or an electron, passes through two slits, it exhibits wave-like behavior, creating an interference pattern on a screen placed behind the slits. However, if one attempts to observe which of the two slits the particle passes through, the interference pattern disappears, and the particle behaves like a classical particle, passing through only one slit. This change in behavior, caused by observation, suggests that the particle exists in a state of superposition until the moment of measurement, when it is "forced" to choose a definite state.

This phenomenon has led physicists and philosophers to ponder the role of consciousness in shaping reality. If observation influences the behavior of quantum particles, what part does the observer's consciousness play in this process? Traditional quantum physics, such as the Copenhagen interpretation proposed by Niels Bohr and Werner Heisenberg, asserts that the properties of particles are not defined until they are measured. This implies that reality at the quantum level does not exist in a definite and concrete sense without the intervention of the observer.

Some scholars, such as John von Neumann and Eugene Wigner, have proposed that consciousness itself might be a fundamental component of the quantum universe. Von Neumann, for example, suggested that the observer's consciousness causes the collapse of the wave function, transitioning from a state of superposition to a definite state. This radical viewpoint implies that the mind not only observes reality but actively contributes to its creation.

The idea that consciousness can influence reality has found resonance outside of quantum physics as well, impacting fields such as the philosophy of mind and psychology. The notion that our thoughts and perceptions can shape the external world is a central principle in many spiritual and philosophical traditions, suggesting a profound connection between mind and matter.

A practical example of how the observer effect can be explored is the famous thought experiment of Schrödinger's cat. This experiment imagines a cat locked in a box with a mechanism that has a 50% chance of killing it based on the decay of a radioactive particle. According to quantum mechanics, as long as the box remains closed, the cat is in a state of superposition, being both alive and dead. Only by opening the box and observing the cat's state does the observer cause the collapse of the wave function, determining the cat's final state. This paradox highlights the crucial role of observation in determining reality.

The implications of the observer effect go beyond quantum physics and touch on fundamental issues about the nature of consciousness and reality. If our mind can influence the quantum world, could it have a similar role in the macroscopic world? This question opens the door to interdisciplinary explorations connecting physics, philosophy, psychology, and neuroscience.

In the context of this book, the observer effect and the role of consciousness provide a theoretical foundation for exploring how our thoughts and perceptions can influence our personal reality. Quantum physics teaches us that reality is not a fixed and immutable entity but a field of possibilities that takes shape through our conscious interaction. We will delve deeper into these ideas in subsequent chapters, showing how we can use our awareness to actively shape our world, living a more conscious and intentional life.

Fundamental Experiments: Schrödinger's Cat and the EPR Paradox

The thought experiments of Schrödinger's cat and the EPR (Einstein-Podolsky-Rosen) paradox are two of the most famous and discussed in the history of quantum physics. Both serve to illustrate the strangeness and profound implications of quantum theories, challenging our understanding of reality and the behavior of subatomic particles.

Schrödinger's cat is a thought experiment proposed by Austrian physicist Erwin Schrödinger in 1935. This experiment imagines a cat locked in a box with a deadly device connected to the decay of a radioactive particle. If the particle decays, the device is activated and kills the cat; if it does not decay, the cat remains alive. According to quantum mechanics, as long as the box remains closed and the state of the cat is not observed, the cat is in a state of superposition, being both alive and dead simultaneously. Only when an observer opens the box and observes the state of the cat does the wave function collapse into a definite state, determining whether the cat is alive or dead.

This thought experiment was conceived by Schrödinger to highlight the apparent absurdity of applying quantum superposition to macroscopic objects. In the subatomic world, particles can exist in multiple states simultaneously, but applying the same concept to a cat seems to defy common sense and our everyday experience of reality. Schrödinger's cat experiment underscores the difficulties in reconciling quantum mechanics with macroscopic reality, emphasizing the need for a deeper understanding of the role of observation and measurement.

The EPR paradox, proposed by Albert Einstein, Boris Podolsky, and Nathan Rosen in 1935, is another thought experiment aimed at questioning the implications of quantum mechanics. The EPR paradox concerns quantum entanglement, a phenomenon where two entangled particles remain correlated regardless of the distance separating them. According to the interpretation of quantum mechanics, if one measures a property of one of the entangled particles, the other particle instantaneously assumes a corresponding value, even if it is at astronomical distances.

Einstein, Podolsky, and Rosen used this paradox to argue that quantum mechanics was incomplete and that there must be local hidden variables to explain the observed correlations. According to them, the idea that one particle could instantaneously influence another at a distance violated the principle of locality and suggested that quantum mechanics did not provide a complete description of physical reality.

The EPR paradox stimulated decades of debates and research. In the 1960s, physicist John Bell developed Bell's inequalities, an experimental test to verify the predictions of quantum mechanics against those of local hidden variable theories. Subsequent experiments, such as those conducted by Alain Aspect in the 1980s, convincingly demonstrated that Bell's inequalities were violated, confirming the predictions of quantum mechanics and suggesting that quantum entanglement is a real and non-local property of the subatomic world.

These fundamental experiments have profound implications for our understanding of the nature of reality. Schrödinger's cat forces us to confront the probabilistic and non-deterministic nature of quantum mechanics, questioning the distinction between the macroscopic and microscopic worlds. The EPR paradox and related experiments show us that the universe is interconnected in ways that challenge our intuitive understanding of space and time.

Ultimately, these thought experiments and their consequences push us to reconsider the role of the observer in the creation of reality and to explore the implications of quantum physics for our understanding of the world and our own existence. These ideas will continue to influence physics, philosophy, and our conceptions of reality for many years to come.

Practical Applications and Emerging Technologies Based on Quantum Physics

Quantum physics, besides being a fascinating and theoretically complex field, has given rise to a series of practical applications and emerging technologies that are revolutionizing our world. These innovations, ranging from quantum computers to quantum cryptography, are opening new frontiers in various sectors, profoundly transforming our daily lives and technological capabilities.

One of the most promising developments is the quantum computer. Unlike classical computers, which use bits to represent information as 0 or 1, quantum computers use qubits, which can exist simultaneously in states of 0, 1, or a superposition of both. This capability allows quantum computers to perform calculations in parallel on an exponential scale, greatly accelerating the resolution of complex problems. For example, optimization problems, molecular simulations, and cryptography can significantly benefit from the computational power of quantum computers. Companies like Google and IBM have already built prototypes of quantum computers, marking the first steps toward a new era of computing.

Quantum cryptography is another revolutionary area. Utilizing the properties of entanglement and superposition, quantum cryptography allows for the creation of cryptographic keys that are theoretically unbreakable. A popular method is the BB84 protocol, which uses quantum states of photons to generate a shared encryption key between two parties. Any attempt to intercept or measure these quantum states alters the data, making the presence of an eavesdropper immediately evident. This technology is already in use in some security applications, such as government and financial communications, promising a future of ultra-secure data transmissions.

In the field of metrology, quantum physics has enabled the development of extremely precise measurement tools. Atomic clocks, which use the frequency of atomic transitions to measure time, are a prime example. These clocks are so precise that they lose only one second every billion years and are essential for the functioning of GPS navigation systems, telecommunications networks, and many other scientific applications.

Quantum physics has also revolutionized the medical field. Technologies based on magnetic resonance, such as nuclear magnetic resonance (NMR) and functional magnetic resonance imaging (fMRI), use quantum principles to visualize and study the interior of the human body in detail. These non-invasive techniques are crucial for early disease diagnosis, treatment planning, and neuroscience research.

Quantum photonics is also emerging as a field of great interest, with applications ranging from telecommunications to computing. Entangled photons can be used to create quantum communication networks that are secure and fast, as well as to enhance information processing in optical quantum computers. This could lead to a quantum internet, a global communication network based on quantum principles that could transform data transmission.

In the energy sector, quantum physics is opening new possibilities. For example, artificial photosynthesis, which relies on the quantum understanding of energy transfer in natural processes, could lead to significant developments in renewable energy production. Researchers are trying to replicate the quantum processes occurring in plants to create new materials and technologies that improve energy efficiency.

Finally, quantum physics is also influencing the field of advanced materials. Scientists are developing quantum materials with unique properties, such as high-temperature superconductors, which could revolutionize electric power transmission and improve the efficiency of electronic devices.

In summary, the practical applications and emerging technologies based on quantum physics are transforming a wide range of sectors, offering innovative and powerful solutions that promise to redefine the future. These developments not only underscore the importance of quantum physics but also show how theoretical principles can translate into tangible advances that enhance our daily lives

Chapter 3

Neuroscience of Perception and Consciousness

Structure and Functioning of the Human Brain

The human brain is an extraordinary and complex organ, composed of approximately 86 billion neurons, each capable of forming thousands of synaptic connections. This intricate neural network not only allows us to think, feel, and act but is also the seat of our consciousness, memories, and emotions. Understanding the structure and functioning of the brain is fundamental to exploring the connections between neuroscience, cognitive psychology, and quantum physics.

Anatomically, the brain can be divided into different regions, each with specific functions. The brain consists primarily of two cerebral hemispheres, connected by the corpus callosum, a thick band of nerve fibers that enables communication between the two sides. Each hemisphere controls opposite functions of the body; for example, the left hemisphere is generally responsible for language and analytical abilities, while the right hemisphere is associated with creativity and spatial information processing.

The cerebral cortex, the outer layer of the brain, is divided into four main lobes: frontal, parietal, temporal, and occipital. The frontal lobe is involved in critical thinking, planning, movement, and social behavior. It is the seat of executive functions, which include decision-making, problem-solving, and impulse control. The parietal lobe integrates sensory information from various parts of the body, helping us understand and respond to our environment. The temporal lobe is crucial for auditory processing and memory, while the occipital lobe is primarily responsible for vision.

Beneath the cerebral cortex, we find essential structures such as the thalamus, hypothalamus, hippocampus, and amygdala. The thalamus acts as a relay center for sensory information, sending inputs to the appropriate cortical lobes. The hypothalamus regulates vital functions such as hunger, thirst, body temperature, and the biological clock. The hippocampus is essential for the formation and retrieval of long-term memories, while the amygdala plays a key role in managing emotions, particularly fear and aggression.

A fascinating aspect of the brain is its plasticity, the ability to change and adapt in response to experiences.

This characteristic, known as neuroplasticity, means that neural connections can be strengthened or weakened, and new connections can form throughout life. Neuroplasticity underlies learning, memory, and recovery after brain injuries. It is also an example of how our thoughts and behaviors can physically influence the structure of our brain.

At the microscopic level, the brain functions through communication between neurons via synapses, specialized junctions where the transfer of electrical and chemical signals occurs. When a neuron transmits a signal, an electrical impulse travels along its axon until it reaches the synapse, where it triggers the release of neurotransmitters. These chemical messengers cross the synaptic gap and bind to receptors on the postsynaptic neuron, generating a new electrical impulse. This complex and rapid process allows the brain to process and respond to an incredible amount of information in real time.

Glial cells, the support cells in the brain, also play crucial roles. They maintain homeostasis, form myelin, which insulates axons and facilitates the rapid transmission of nerve impulses, and provide support and protection to neurons. Glial cells also contribute to the repair and regeneration of nervous tissue, demonstrating the importance of cellular interactions in maintaining brain function.

Understanding the structure and functioning of the brain not only helps us grasp the biological foundations of the mind and behavior but also paves the way for new therapies for neurological and psychiatric diseases. As we discover more about how the brain processes information and adapts, we can develop more effective approaches to promote mental health and well-being, leveraging the intrinsic potential of our brain.

Mechanisms of Sensory Perception and Information Interpretation

The mechanisms of sensory perception and information interpretation are fundamental processes that allow the human brain to understand and interact with the surrounding world. These processes involve a complex network of neurons and neural pathways that transform external stimuli into meaningful perceptual experiences.

Sensory perception begins with specialized sensory receptors present in our sense organs: eyes, ears, skin, nose, and tongue. These receptors are designed to detect specific types of stimuli: light for vision, sound waves for hearing, chemicals for smell and taste, and pressure and temperature for touch. When these receptors are stimulated, they generate nerve impulses that are transmitted to the brain via sensory nerves.

Take vision, for example. Light enters the eye through the cornea and lens, which focus it onto the retina. The retina contains millions of photoreceptors, rods, and cones, which convert light energy into electrical signals. These signals are then transmitted to the optic nerve and finally to the brain, where they are processed by the visual cortex located in the occipital lobe. Here, the brain reconstructs the visual image, allowing us to recognize shapes, colors, and movements.

Hearing follows a similar process but involves the transformation of sound waves into electrical impulses. Sound waves are collected by the outer ear and funneled into the ear canal, where they cause the eardrum to vibrate. These vibrations are transmitted through a series of tiny bones in the middle ear to the cochlea in the inner ear. The cochlea, a spiral-shaped structure, contains hair cells that convert the vibrations into nerve impulses. These impulses are sent to the auditory nerve and then to the auditory cortex in the temporal lobe of the brain, where they are interpreted as sounds.

Touch, smell, and taste follow analogous pathways, each with their own specialized receptors and neural pathways to specific areas of the brain. For example, tactile receptors in the skin detect pressure, temperature, and pain, sending signals to the central nervous system through spinal nerves. These signals are processed by the somatosensory cortex in the parietal lobe, allowing us to perceive and respond to tactile stimuli.

Once sensory stimuli have been converted into nerve impulses and transmitted to the brain, the process of information interpretation comes into play. This process is highly complex and involves the integration of signals from different sensory modalities, as well as the use of memory, attention, and cognitive expectations. Our final perceptual experience is a combination of raw sensory data and cognitive interpretations that give meaning to this data.

For example, when we see an object, our brain not only processes visual characteristics such as shape, color, and size but also uses memory to recognize the object and assign meaning to it. This recognition process is influenced by our past experiences, acquired knowledge, and the context in which the object is located. If we see an apple, our brain quickly recognizes it as an edible fruit based on previous experiences and knowledge.

Attention plays a crucial role in the interpretation of information. Our brain constantly receives a vast amount of sensory stimuli, but we can only attend to a portion of them. Attention allows us to focus on relevant information and filter out irrelevant ones, thus enhancing our ability to interact effectively with the environment.

In summary, the mechanisms of sensory perception and information interpretation represent an extraordinary dance of detection, transmission, and processing that allows us to navigate the world. These processes not only enable us to perceive our environment but also to interact with it in a meaningful and conscious way. Understanding these mechanisms offers a window into how our brain constructs our perceptual reality and how we can improve our interaction with the world around us.

Consciousness: Definitions and Neuroscientific Theories

Consciousness is one of the most fascinating and complex mysteries in science and philosophy. It represents the core of our subjective experience, the quality that allows us to be aware of ourselves and the world around us. But what exactly do we mean when we talk about consciousness, and how do neuroscientists attempt to explain it?

Defining consciousness is no simple task. In general terms, consciousness can be described as the state of awareness of oneself and the external environment. This definition includes the ability to have thoughts, perceptions, emotions, and intentions. However, the precise nature of consciousness and its underlying mechanisms are still subjects of intense debate and research.

One of the most influential neuroscientific theories is the Integrated Information Theory (IIT) proposed by Giulio Tononi. According to this theory, consciousness corresponds to a system's capacity to integrate information. IIT suggests that consciousness emerges when a system has a high degree of information integration, meaning that the various parts of the system are tightly interconnected and information can be combined meaningfully. This level of integration is quantifiable through a measure called "phi." A system with a high phi value is considered highly conscious.

Another relevant theory is Bernard Baars' Global Workspace Theory (GNWT). This theory proposes that consciousness emerges when information is made available to a "global workspace" in the brain, where it can be shared among different neural areas. GNWT posits that consciousness allows for the global access and distribution of information in the brain, facilitating cognitive functions such as long-term memory, planning, and problem-solving.

Michael Graziano's Attention Schema Theory (AST) offers another interesting approach. Graziano suggests that consciousness is a neural model constructed by the brain to monitor and control attentional processes.

According to this theory, the brain creates a simplified representation of its own attention, allowing it to efficiently direct cognitive resources. Therefore, consciousness is the result of an internal model that the brain uses to monitor and manage its cognitive and perceptual states.

Neuroscience also seeks to locate the neural bases of consciousness through neuroimaging studies and brain lesions. Brain regions such as the thalamus, prefrontal cortex, and parietal areas have been identified as crucial for conscious awareness. The thalamus, in particular, acts as a relay center that directs sensory information to the cerebral cortex, while the prefrontal cortex is involved in planning and controlling conscious actions.

Studies of patients with brain lesions have provided further insights. For example, damage to the primary visual cortex can lead to cortical blindness, in which patients are unaware of visual stimuli despite their ability to respond to them unconsciously. This phenomenon, known as blindsight, suggests that visual consciousness requires the integration of sensory information in the cerebral cortex.

Another relevant field of research is the study of altered states of consciousness, such as sleep, dreams, anesthesia, and near-death experiences. These states offer unique opportunities to explore how consciousness can be modulated and which neural circuits are involved. For example, during REM sleep, the brain shows intense activity similar to that of wakefulness, associated with vivid dreams, suggesting that dream consciousness involves complex neural mechanisms.

In summary, consciousness remains one of the great mysteries of science, but neuroscience is making significant strides toward its understanding. Current theories offer fascinating and promising models, but many fundamental questions remain open. Ongoing neuroscientific exploration not only brings us closer to solving these enigmas but also helps us better understand the nature of our subjective experience and our place in the universe.

How the Brain Creates Reality: Cognitive Maps and Mental Models

The human brain is an incredibly sophisticated machine, capable of constructing a coherent and meaningful representation of the world around us. This process of constructing reality is made possible through cognitive maps and mental models, which the brain develops and uses to interpret and interact with our environment.

Cognitive maps are mental representations of physical spaces, concepts, and the relationships between objects and ideas. These maps allow us to navigate both the physical and conceptual worlds, helping us to understand and remember complex information. For example, when we enter a room, our brain creates a mental map of the arrangement of objects, the people present, and possible exits. This allows us to move and interact effectively without having to consciously analyze every detail.

Mental models, on the other hand, are cognitive structures that represent how things work in the real world. These models allow us to make predictions, solve problems, and understand cause and effect. For example, our mental model of how a car works helps us drive without having to consciously think about every single action required to do so.

The process through which the brain creates these maps and models is fascinating and complex. It involves the integration of sensory information, cognitive processing, and memory. Information gathered by our senses is sent to the brain, where it is processed and compared with preexisting knowledge. This comparison allows the brain to constantly update its cognitive maps and mental models, thereby improving our ability to understand and predict the world.

A crucial component of this process is perception. Perception is not a mere reflection of external reality but an active interpretation by the brain. For example, our eyes receive light signals that are converted into electrical impulses and sent to the visual cortex. Here, these signals are processed and integrated with previous information, creating a coherent visual representation. This process allows the brain to compensate for variations in lighting conditions, recognize objects from different angles, and perceive depth and movement.

Memory plays a fundamental role in the construction of reality. Our past experiences influence how we interpret new information. For example, if we have learned that a certain type of fruit is edible, our brain will use this knowledge to quickly and correctly interpret future encounters with the same fruit. This process of association and recognition is made possible by neural circuits that connect different areas of the brain, allowing for the rapid integration of sensory information and previous memories.

Attention is another key element in the construction of reality. Since the brain receives an enormous amount of sensory information at every moment, it must select which information to process and which to ignore. Attention allows us to focus on what is relevant, enhancing our ability to respond effectively to stimuli. For example, when driving a car, our attention selects relevant information such as the position of other vehicles, road signs, and road conditions, filtering out irrelevant distractions.

Mental models not only help us understand the external world but also influence our behavior and decisions. For example, our mental model of a social environment guides our interactions with others, allowing us to anticipate their reactions and adapt our behavior accordingly. These models are flexible and can be modified in response to new experiences and information.

In summary, the brain creates our reality through a dynamic and complex process that involves sensory processing, memory, attention, and the construction of cognitive maps and mental models. These mental tools allow us to navigate the world effectively, understand complex relationships, and make informed decisions. Understanding these processes provides us with a fascinating insight into how our mind constructs and interprets reality, allowing us to live in a world rich with meaning and possibilities.

Examples of How Perception Can Be Altered or Manipulated

Perception, being the result of complex brain processes, can be altered or manipulated in various ways, often with surprising and revealing effects on how our brain interprets reality. Here are some examples that illustrate how perception can be distorted or deceived, offering a fascinating window into the nature of our mind.

A classic example of altered perception is the optical illusion. Optical illusions exploit the ways in which the brain processes visual information, leading us to see something that does not correspond to physical reality. Take the Müller-Lyer illusion, where two lines of the same length appear different due to the arrows at their ends. This illusion works because the brain uses contextual clues to judge the length of the lines, demonstrating how perception is an interpretative process rather than a mere recording of visual information.

Another example of perceptual manipulation is found in experiences of synesthesia, a condition where stimulation of one sense causes automatic and involuntary experiences in another sense. For example, a person with synesthesia might "see" specific colors when hearing certain sounds or "taste" flavors when reading words. This condition, which affects a small percentage of the population, demonstrates the brain's extraordinary plasticity and its ability to create unusual connections between different sensory modalities.

Perception can also be influenced by selective attention, a phenomenon explored in the famous "invisible gorilla" experiment conducted by Christopher Chabris and Daniel Simons. In this experiment, participants are asked to watch a video of a group of people passing a basketball and count how many times the ball is passed. During the video, a person in a gorilla suit walks through the scene, beating their chest. Surprisingly, many participants do not notice the gorilla, focused as they are on counting the passes. This experiment demonstrates how our attention can be so focused on a specific task that we ignore relevant and unusual elements in our visual field.

Perception can also be altered through the use of psychoactive substances. Drugs such as LSD, psilocybin, and mescaline can induce hallucinations, altering our perception of time, space, and reality. These experiences can include visions of vivid colors, distorted shapes, and amplified sensations, revealing how brain chemistry profoundly influences our sensory experience. Hallucinations can also occur in medical conditions like schizophrenia, where altered perceptions can become an integral part of the patient's daily life.

Sensory deprivation can also manipulate perception. In sensory deprivation experiments, where a person is isolated from all external stimuli, the brain can begin to create internal stimuli to compensate for the lack of input. This can lead to hallucinatory experiences, demonstrating how much our perception depends on continuous interaction with the external environment.

Another example is the effects of context and expectations. Perception can be strongly influenced by what we expect to see or hear. In a famous experiment, participants were asked to taste wines labeled with different prices. In reality, it was the same wine, but participants rated the more expensive wine as higher quality. This shows how our expectations can alter our perceptual experience, leading us to interpret stimuli in ways that align with our preconceived beliefs.

Finally, emerging technologies such as virtual reality (VR) and augmented reality (AR) offer new possibilities for perceptual manipulation. These technologies can create immersive environments that completely alter our perception of the world, allowing us to experience alternative realities. The use of VR and AR in therapy, education, and entertainment demonstrates how we can use our understanding of perceptions to enhance our experiences and solve complex problems.

In summary, perception is a highly dynamic and flexible process, easily influenced by a variety of internal and external factors. The examples of how perception can be altered or manipulated show us not only the complexity of the human brain but also the possibilities for exploring and better understanding our subjective reality.

Chapter 4

Cognitive Psychology: Thoughts and Beliefs

The Foundations of Cognitive Psychology: Mental Processes and Functioning

Cognitive psychology is a fascinating field that focuses on the study of mental processes, exploring how people perceive, think, remember, and learn. This discipline developed in the mid-20th century as a response to behaviorism, which focused exclusively on observable behavior while neglecting internal mental processes. Cognitive psychology, in contrast, recognizes that understanding the mind is essential to explaining human behavior.

One of the key concepts in cognitive psychology is the information processor model, which likens the human mind to a computer. This model suggests that the brain receives, processes, stores, and retrieves information in a manner similar to how a computer processes data. Mental processes are viewed as a series of sequential operations that transform sensory inputs into behavioral outputs. This approach has led to the development of detailed models that describe how information is processed from initial perception to final response.

A central element of cognitive psychology is the study of memory, which is generally divided into three main stages: encoding, storage, and retrieval. Encoding involves transforming information into a format that can be stored in the brain. For example, when we read a book, our brain encodes the words and sentences into meaningful concepts that we can remember. Storage refers to maintaining this information over time. Short-term memory, or working memory, is limited and retains information only for brief periods, while long-term memory can store information for years or even a lifetime. Retrieval is the process of accessing stored information when needed, such as recalling an answer during an exam or reminiscing about a childhood memory.

Another key area of cognitive psychology is attention, which involves selecting relevant information from the environment. Since our brain cannot process all incoming sensory information simultaneously, attention allows us to focus on what is important at any given moment. Selective attention helps us filter out distractions and concentrate on specific tasks, such as listening to a conversation in a crowded room or reading a book in a noisy environment.

Cognitive psychology also explores thinking and problem-solving, studying how people use information to make decisions and solve puzzles. This includes how individuals formulate hypotheses, make inferences, and use strategies to tackle new or complex situations. For example, divergent thinking, which generates creative and original ideas, is crucial for innovation and creative problem-solving.

Language is another central theme in cognitive psychology. Researchers examine how people understand, produce, and use language to communicate. This includes the syntax, semantics, and pragmatics of language, as well as how the brain processes linguistic information. Theories of cognitive linguistics aim to explain how language is acquired, developed, and used, revealing deep connections between thought and language.

Finally, cognitive psychology is interested in emotions and how they influence cognitive processes. Emotions not only affect our mental state but can also modulate attention, memory, and decision-making. For instance, anxiety can reduce the ability to concentrate and recall information, while happiness can enhance creativity and problem-solving ability.

In summary, cognitive psychology provides a deep understanding of the mental processes that drive our behavior. By exploring how we perceive, think, remember, and learn, this discipline helps us better understand the complexity of the human mind and develop strategies to improve learning, memory, and problem-solving in daily life. The richness of research in this field continues to reveal new insights, paving the way for innovations in education, therapy, and technology.

How Thoughts Influence Emotions and Behaviors

Thoughts are the core of our inner world and have a significant influence on our emotions and behaviors. The relationship between thoughts, emotions, and behaviors is a central area of cognitive psychology and cognitive-behavioral therapy, offering valuable insights into how our minds function.

Our thoughts, which can be conscious or automatic, act as a filter through which we interpret experiences. When we encounter a situation, our brain quickly analyzes the available information and forms thoughts or beliefs about what is happening. These thoughts directly influence how we feel emotionally. For example, if we interpret a social situation as a rejection, we might feel sad or anxious. Conversely, if we interpret the same situation as a new opportunity, we might feel excited and motivated.

The cognitive theory proposed by Aaron Beck posits that distorted or irrational thoughts can lead to negative emotions and dysfunctional behaviors. These distorted thoughts, known as cognitive distortions, include patterns of thinking such as all-or-nothing thinking, catastrophizing, and personalization. For example, a person who has experienced a minor failure might think, "I never do anything right," an example of all-or-nothing thinking. This negative thought can lead to feelings of hopelessness and avoidance behaviors.

Emotions, in turn, influence our behaviors. When dominated by negative emotions such as fear or sadness, we are more likely to avoid situations or withdraw socially. These behaviors can further reinforce negative thoughts, creating a negative feedback loop. For instance, if a person feels anxious about public speaking and decides to avoid the event, the temporary relief reinforces the thought that public speaking is dangerous, increasing anxiety for future similar situations.

Conversely, positive thoughts can generate positive emotions and productive behaviors. Thoughts like "I can handle this challenge" or "I have overcome difficult situations in the past" can instill confidence and hope, leading to proactive and successful behaviors. These positive behaviors, in turn, reinforce positive thoughts, creating a virtuous cycle.

Cognitive-behavioral therapy (CBT) leverages this relationship between thoughts, emotions, and behaviors to help individuals modify dysfunctional thinking patterns and develop more effective strategies. Through techniques such as cognitive restructuring, therapists help patients identify and modify distorted thoughts, promoting a more realistic and positive view of their experiences. For example, a person who believes they are destined to fail might be guided to examine evidence of past successes, helping them develop a more balanced and encouraging view of themselves.

Furthermore, self-observation and awareness are powerful tools for understanding and modifying the relationship between thoughts, emotions, and behaviors. Practices such as mindfulness help individuals become more aware of their automatic thoughts and emotional reactions, allowing them to respond more deliberately and less reactively. Awareness enables us to recognize when our thoughts are becoming negative or distorted, offering us the opportunity to intervene and change our perspective before it negatively impacts our emotions and behaviors.

The neuroplasticity of the brain plays a crucial role in this process of change. When we modify our thoughts and behaviors, we create new neural connections and strengthen existing ones. This process of neural remodeling demonstrates how cognitive and behavioral change can have lasting and beneficial effects on our mental health and overall well-being.

Ultimately, understanding how thoughts influence emotions and behaviors provides us with powerful tools to improve our lives. Through awareness, cognitive restructuring, and the practice of positive thinking, we can break negative cycles and promote greater emotional resilience, well-being, and personal success. This process not only enhances our quality of life but also enables us to face challenges with greater confidence and optimism, transforming the way we live and interact with the world.

The Power of Beliefs: Placebo, Nocebo, and Self-Fulfilling Prophecies

Beliefs have an extraordinary power to shape our experience of the world, influencing not only our mental state but also our physiology. This power is particularly evident in the phenomena of placebo, nocebo, and self-fulfilling prophecies, which demonstrate how expectations and convictions can concretely alter our reality.

The term "placebo effect" refers to clinical improvements observed when a patient receives an inert treatment but believes it to be effective. This phenomenon has been extensively documented in clinical studies where patients taking sugar pills, believing them to be real medications, reported significant improvements in their symptoms. The placebo effect is not just psychological; it can also induce real physiological changes in the body. For example, patients who believe they have taken a painkiller may experience an actual reduction in pain due to the release of endorphins, the body's natural pain relievers.

The nocebo effect is the "dark twin" of the placebo. It occurs when negative expectations lead to worsening symptoms or new symptoms after an inert treatment. If a patient believes that a harmless drug will have negative side effects, they are highly likely to experience them. This demonstrates how deeply beliefs can influence not only the mind but also the body. The nocebo effect highlights the importance of carefully managing patient communication and expectations in the medical field.

Self-fulfilling prophecies are another example of the power of beliefs. A self-fulfilling prophecy occurs when a person holds a belief or expectation that influences their behavior in such a way that the belief becomes a reality. This phenomenon has been studied in various contexts, including education, work, and personal relationships. For example, if a teacher believes that a particular student is highly intelligent, they might unconsciously provide more attention and support to that student, thereby improving the student's academic performance. This effect is known as the Pygmalion effect and shows how expectations can influence the behavior of others.

These phenomena share a common principle: beliefs and expectations shape our perception and interaction with reality. This happens through deeply interconnected psychological and physiological mechanisms. Our mind is not a mere passive observer but an active participant that shapes our experiences through the filter of beliefs.

The power of beliefs is also the basis for many therapeutic and healing practices. Cognitive-behavioral therapy, for example, is based on the idea that by changing dysfunctional beliefs, significant changes can be achieved in emotions and behaviors. Similarly, techniques like meditation and positive visualization harness the power of beliefs to promote health and well-being.

Furthermore, understanding the power of beliefs has profound implications for our daily lives. Being aware of our beliefs and expectations allows us to reflect on how they influence our actions and outcomes. We can learn to cultivate positive and realistic beliefs that help us achieve our goals and improve our quality of life.

In conclusion, the phenomena of placebo, nocebo, and self-fulfilling prophecies show us that beliefs are not just abstract ideas in our minds but powerful forces that shape our reality. Understanding and harnessing the power of beliefs can lead to significant improvements in health, well-being, and personal success, demonstrating that the mind is a powerful and transformative tool.

Cognitive Theories of Motivation and Personal Change

Cognitive theories of motivation and personal change provide a deep understanding of how our thoughts, beliefs, and expectations influence our actions and our ability to transform ourselves. These theories explore the internal forces that drive us to pursue goals and modify behaviors, offering valuable tools for making significant changes in our lives.

One of the most influential theories is the Self-Determination Theory (SDT) developed by Edward Deci and Richard Ryan. SDT posits that human motivation is driven by three fundamental psychological needs: autonomy, competence, and relatedness. Autonomy refers to the desire to be the agent of one's own actions and decisions. Competence involves the need to feel effective and capable in one's activities. Relatedness is the need to feel connected to others and to have meaningful relationships. When these needs are met, we are intrinsically motivated to engage in activities that promote our well-being and personal growth.

Another fundamental theory is the Goal Setting Theory by Edwin Locke and Gary Latham, which explores how goal-setting influences motivation and performance. According to this theory, clear and specific goals, accompanied by regular feedback, are essential for maintaining high motivation. Goals must be challenging yet achievable, which stimulates commitment and perseverance. Additionally, the goal-setting process must include a component of self-efficacy, the belief in one's ability to achieve these goals.

Albert Bandura's Self-Efficacy Theory plays a crucial role in personal change. Bandura suggests that our perception of self-efficacy, or the confidence in our ability to perform specific behaviors necessary to achieve desired outcomes, greatly influences our motivation and actions. People with high self-efficacy are more likely to view difficult tasks as challenges to be mastered rather than threats to be avoided. This positive attitude promotes resilience and persistence in the face of difficulties, facilitating personal change.

Another important concept is Mindset, developed by Carol Dweck. Dweck distinguishes between two types of mindsets: fixed mindset and growth mindset.

People with a fixed mindset believe their abilities are static and unchangeable. Consequently, they avoid challenges for fear of failure and proving their incompetence. In contrast, people with a growth mindset believe their abilities can be developed through effort and practice. This drives them to embrace challenges, learn from failures, and see effort as a path to mastery. Adopting a growth mindset is fundamental for personal change, as it encourages continuous learning and adaptation.

The Intrinsic and Extrinsic Motivation Theory is also central to understanding motivation. Intrinsic motivation comes from within, from the pleasure and satisfaction derived from the activity itself. Conversely, extrinsic motivation is driven by external factors, such as rewards or social pressures. Research shows that while extrinsic motivation can be effective in the short term, intrinsic motivation leads to more enduring commitment and significant personal change.

Finally, the Expectancy-Value Theory by Martin Fishbein and Icek Ajzen combines cognitive and behavioral aspects to explain motivation. This theory suggests that our motivation to perform an action is influenced by our expectations of success and the value we place on the outcome. If we believe we can achieve a goal and consider it important, we are more motivated to engage in it.

In summary, cognitive theories of motivation and personal change provide a comprehensive framework for understanding how our thoughts and beliefs influence our behavior and ability to change. Understanding these principles can help us develop more effective strategies to achieve our goals and improve our lives, promoting continuous and lasting personal growth.

Techniques for Changing Limiting Thoughts and Beliefs

Changing limiting thoughts and beliefs is a crucial step towards enhancing personal well-being and achieving goals. These thoughts and beliefs, often rooted in childhood or stemming from negative experiences, can hinder personal progress and success. Fortunately, there are several effective techniques for transforming these limiting beliefs into empowering thoughts.

One widely used technique is cognitive restructuring, a process from cognitive-behavioral therapy (CBT) that helps individuals identify and modify distorted thoughts. The first step involves recognizing the automatic negative thoughts that arise in response to specific situations. These thoughts are often irrational and based on distorted perceptions of reality. Once identified, they can be critically analyzed by questioning whether they are based on real facts or represent dysfunctional thinking patterns. Replacing these thoughts with more realistic and positive alternatives can lead to improved associated emotions and behaviors.

Another powerful technique is the practice of mindfulness. Mindfulness involves being fully present in the moment, observing one's thoughts and feelings without judgment. This practice can help increase awareness of limiting thoughts and distance oneself from them, recognizing them as mere products of the mind rather than absolute truths. Over time, mindfulness can reduce the impact of negative thoughts and increase the ability to respond more balanced and thoughtfully to life's challenges.

Visualization is another effective technique for changing limiting beliefs. Vividly imagining situations where one successfully faces and overcomes fears or insecurities can help alter self-perception and capabilities. This technique works because the brain does not clearly distinguish between real and imagined experiences; therefore, mentally practicing success can enhance confidence and self-efficacy.

Positive affirmations are simple yet powerful tools for reframing negative thoughts. Repeating positive and motivating affirmations can help replace limiting beliefs with new empowering convictions. For example, replacing a thought like "I can't do this" with

"I am capable of facing this challenge successfully" can gradually transform self-perception and improve behavior.

Journaling, or keeping a diary, is another useful technique. Regularly writing down thoughts and feelings allows for reflection and identification of limiting thought patterns. Through journaling, one can critically examine beliefs and track progress in changing them. This practice also provides a safe space to explore and better understand one's emotions and motivations.

Values work is a technique that involves identifying and aligning actions with one's deepest personal values. Often, limiting beliefs conflict with core values. Recognizing this conflict and choosing to act in ways that reflect personal values can help overcome limiting beliefs and lead to a more authentic and fulfilling life.

Another approach is the ABCDE method, developed by Albert Ellis as part of rational emotive behavior therapy (REBT). This method involves five steps:

Identifying the Activating Event (A).

Identifying the Belief (B) about this event.

Recognizing the emotional Consequences (C) of this belief.

Disputing (D) the belief by questioning its validity.

Replacing the belief with a new Effective (E) belief that is more realistic and helpful.

Incorporating these techniques into daily routines can lead to significant changes in how challenges are perceived and addressed. Limiting beliefs are not destined to be permanent; with commitment and practice, they can be transformed into beliefs that promote success and well-being. This process of transformation requires time and patience, but the results can be profoundly liberating and empowering.

Chapter 5

The Theory of Attraction and Quantum Connections

Principles of the Theory of Attraction: Focus, Intention, and Vibration

The theory of attraction is a captivating concept that has fascinated many in the world of personal development and spirituality. It is based on the idea that our thoughts, emotions, and beliefs directly influence the experiences we attract into our lives. The fundamental principles of this theory are focus, intention, and vibration, which together create a powerful formula for manifesting desires and transforming reality.

Focus represents the mental concentration and attention we give to certain thoughts and goals. According to the theory of attraction, what we focus on tends to expand and manifest in our lives. This principle is based on the idea that the brain acts like a magnet, attracting events and circumstances that align with our dominant thoughts. When we intensely focus on a desire, we send a clear and powerful signal to the universe. This concentrated focus helps to filter opportunities and resources necessary to achieve our goals, creating a mental map that guides us towards success.

Intention is the second crucial principle of the theory of attraction. Intention goes beyond mere desire; it involves a conscious and determined decision to create something in one's life. It is the act of deliberately directing mental and emotional energy towards a specific goal. When we formulate a clear intention, we establish a direction for our actions and behaviors. Intention acts as an internal compass, keeping us aligned with our desires and motivating us to take the necessary actions to realize them. It is the driving force that transforms thoughts into tangible reality.

Vibration is the third principle and refers to the energetic frequency of our emotions and thoughts. Every thought and feeling emits a certain vibration, which can be high or low. High vibrations are associated with positive emotions such as love, joy, and gratitude, while low vibrations are linked to negative emotions such as fear, anger, and sadness. According to the theory of attraction, we attract into our lives what vibrates at the same frequency as our predominant emotions and thoughts. Therefore, maintaining a high vibration is essential for attracting positive and desirable experiences.

To put these principles into practice, it is crucial to cultivate awareness of one's thoughts and emotions. For instance, practicing gratitude can elevate our vibrations and attract more reasons for gratitude. Visualizing our goals with clarity and feeling can strengthen focus and intention, creating a powerful combination of mental and emotional energy. Additionally, taking action aligned with our intentions is crucial. It is not enough to think positively; we must also take concrete actions that reflect our desires and beliefs.

The theory of attraction also emphasizes the importance of releasing internal resistances, such as doubts and fears, which can block the flow of positive energy. Techniques such as meditation, self-reflection, and therapy can help identify and overcome these barriers, allowing for greater fluidity in manifesting desires.

In summary, the theory of attraction offers a powerful perspective on how our thoughts, intentions, and vibrations can shape our reality. Understanding and applying these principles can transform our lives, helping us consciously create experiences that resonate with our deepest dreams and aspirations. Through focus, intention, and vibration, we can become the architects of our destiny, tapping into the power of the mind to manifest a life of abundance and fulfillment.

How Quantum Physics Concepts Support the Theory of Attraction

Quantum physics, with its revolutionary and counterintuitive theories, offers a fascinating framework that can support the theory of attraction in surprising ways. Although quantum physics and the theory of attraction belong to different scientific and philosophical domains, the analogies between their principles provide fertile ground for understanding how our thoughts can influence reality.

One of the key concepts of quantum physics that resonates with the theory of attraction is the principle of superposition. In quantum terms, a particle can exist in multiple states simultaneously until it is observed. This idea suggests that all possible realities coexist simultaneously and that the act of observing or focusing attention on a specific state collapses the wave function into that particular reality. Similarly, the theory of attraction asserts that focusing on a specific desire can lead to its manifestation. When we focus our thoughts and emotions on a goal, we are, in a way, choosing that reality among the many possibilities, attracting it into our experience.

Quantum entanglement is another concept that offers an intriguing parallel with the theory of attraction. Entanglement describes a phenomenon where two particles, once entangled, remain connected regardless of the distance that separates them. A change in the state of one particle instantly influences the state of the other. This phenomenon seems to violate the principle of locality and suggests that connections can exist at a deep, non-local level. The theory of attraction posits that thoughts and emotions emit vibrations that can influence the environment and attract similar experiences. The idea that our minds can create invisible connections with the external world through mental energy finds an echo in quantum entanglement, where particles remain in a state of connection beyond space and time.

Heisenberg's uncertainty principle, which states that it is impossible to simultaneously and precisely know both the position and velocity of a particle, introduces the idea that observation affects the behavior of particles themselves. This suggests that reality at the quantum level is not fixed but can be influenced by the observer. Similarly, the theory of attraction emphasizes that our thoughts and intentions influence the reality we experience. Our attention and beliefs act as the observer that modifies subatomic reality, shaping the circumstances of our daily lives.

The observer effect in quantum physics further reinforces this connection. Experiments have shown that the act of observing a quantum particle changes its state. This principle aligns with the idea that focused attention and conscious intention can influence and create our reality. When we concentrate on a goal with clarity and conviction, we are essentially "observing" that desired reality, facilitating its manifestation.

Quantum physics, therefore, offers a language and conceptual structure that can explain how thoughts and emotions might influence the physical world. While traditional science might be cautious about directly linking quantum physics to the theory of attraction, the analogies between quantum principles and those of manifestation are striking and intriguing.

In this context, we can see how the human mind, with its ability to focus, intend, and vibrate, acts as a powerful tool of creation. Quantum physics teaches us that reality is not fixed and deterministic but a dynamic field of possibilities influenced by the observer. This opens new perspectives on how we can use our awareness and thinking to actively shape our lives, realizing our desires through a deep and conscious interaction with the universe.

Examples of Invisible Connections in Daily Life and History

The theory of attraction and the concepts of quantum physics may seem abstract, but they become tangible when we observe them in the invisible connections that permeate daily life and history. These examples illustrate how thoughts, intentions, and vibrations have influenced events and circumstances, offering a fascinating perspective on how our minds can interact with the world.

One of the most well-known examples in daily life is the experience of thinking intensely about someone and shortly after receiving a call or message from that person. This phenomenon, often dismissed as coincidence, can be seen as a reflection of the invisible connections that exist between minds. It is as if our thoughts emit a sort of "signal" that can be received by the other person, creating a connection that manifests in the physical world.

Another everyday example is the effect that our emotions have on our social interactions. When we enter a room with a positive vibration, such as joy or enthusiasm, we notice that the people around us respond positively, creating a pleasant and welcoming atmosphere. Conversely, a negative vibration, such as anger or sadness, can negatively influence the environment, creating tension and discomfort. These examples demonstrate how our emotional vibrations can influence the experiences and reactions of others, supporting the idea that we are all connected on an energetic level.

History is also rich with examples of invisible connections. Consider the famous dream of Dmitri

Mendeleev, the Russian chemist who dreamt of the periodic table of elements. Mendeleev was intensely working to organize the chemical elements into a coherent system. After days of frustration, he dreamt of a table where all the elements fell into their natural place. Upon waking, he transcribed the dream, giving birth to the periodic table. This event can be seen as an example of how intense focus and intention can lead to insights that seem to come from a higher level of awareness, connecting the dreamer's mind to a universal source of knowledge.

Another historical example is the discovery of the structure of DNA by James Watson and Francis Crick. Although their discovery was the result of rigorous scientific research, both have spoken of moments of sudden insight, almost as if the solution had revealed itself to them. This phenomenon of scientific "serendipity" can be seen as an example of how the mind, through focus and intention, can connect to a broader field of knowledge, leading to revolutionary discoveries.

In the world of the arts, many artists talk about a creative flow where ideas seem to emerge spontaneously, almost as if they were channeled from an external source. Writers, musicians, and painters often describe moments of inspiration where they feel they are simply the medium through which the work comes to life. This sense of connection with a universal creative source is another example of how invisible connections influence our ability to create and innovate.

Invisible connections also manifest in collective movements and social transformations. Consider historical changes like the civil rights movement in the United States or the fall of the Berlin Wall. These events were catalyzed not only by political actions but also by a shift in collective consciousness. Ideas of freedom, justice, and unity resonated deeply in the minds and hearts of millions of people, creating a collective vibration that made change possible.

These examples show that invisible connections, supported by the principles of the theory of attraction and quantum physics, are not just theoretical ideas but real phenomena that influence our daily lives and history. Recognizing and understanding these connections offers us a broader and deeper perspective on the nature of reality and the power of the human mind.

Criticism and Controversies Surrounding the Theory of Attraction

The theory of attraction, despite its popularity and allure, is not without its critics and controversies. Many skeptics and scholars have raised doubts about its scientific validity and practical efficacy, highlighting several weaknesses that deserve careful consideration.

One of the most common criticisms concerns the lack of rigorous scientific evidence supporting the theory of attraction. Detractors argue that much of the evidence in favor of the theory is anecdotal and does not withstand rigorous scientific scrutiny. While some individuals may indeed report positive experiences attributed to the use of the theory of attraction, skeptics maintain that these successes can be explained by other factors, such as positive psychology, the placebo effect, or simply personal perseverance. The correlation between positive thinking and success does not necessarily imply direct causation, a point frequently emphasized by critics.

Another controversy revolves around the potential responsibility and blame the theory of attraction may impose on individuals. According to this theory, people attract into their lives what they focus on and what they emit in terms of energetic vibrations. This implies that even negative experiences are the result of negative thoughts and vibrations. Critics and psychologists warn that this view can be harmful, as it may lead individuals to feel guilty or responsible for their misfortunes, such as serious illnesses or accidents, when in reality, these events may be beyond their control.

The theory of attraction has also been criticized for its oversimplification. Skeptics argue that reducing personal success and the achievement of complex goals to a formula based solely on positive thinking and energetic vibrations is naive. Reality, they contend, is much more complex and multifactorial, and success depends on a combination of internal and external factors, including skills, opportunities, socioeconomic resources, and social support. Ignoring these variables can lead to a superficial and reductive interpretation of the dynamics of success and failure.

Another significant criticism concerns the potential commercial exploitation of the theory of attraction. In recent decades, the theory has become a cornerstone of a lucrative industry that includes books, seminars, online courses, and various products. Some critics claim that this commercialization exploits people's hopes and desires without offering real long-term benefits. The promise of transforming one's life through simple positive thinking techniques can be enticing, but it often fails to deliver the lasting results that are promised.

Finally, there are ethical concerns regarding the theory of attraction. Some argue that focusing exclusively on one's desires and personal goals may promote a selfish and individualistic attitude. In a world that increasingly requires collaboration, empathy, and collective action to address global challenges such as climate change, social inequality, and health crises, the theory of attraction could be seen as encouraging an egocentric attitude.

Despite these criticisms, it is important to acknowledge that the theory of attraction has also had a positive impact on many people, helping them develop a more optimistic and proactive mindset. However, it is essential to maintain a balanced and critical approach, recognizing both the potential benefits and the limitations and risks associated with this theory. The key may lie in integrating the principles of the theory of attraction with a broader and more nuanced understanding of reality, considering the complexity of human experiences and the multiple variables that influence success and well-being.

By doing so, individuals can harness the positive aspects of the theory while remaining grounded in a realistic perspective that acknowledges the multifaceted nature of life and the myriad factors that contribute to achieving one's goals and overall happiness.

Practical Strategies for Applying the Law of Attraction in Personal Life

Applying the law of attraction in personal life may seem like an abstract concept, but there are practical strategies that can help integrate these principles into daily life. These techniques can enhance our ability to attract what we desire, improve overall well-being, and promote greater personal fulfillment.

One of the first strategies is the practice of creative visualization. This technique involves vividly and detailedly imagining your goals as if they were already realized. During visualization, it is important to engage all senses: seeing, hearing, touching, and even smelling and tasting what you desire. For example, if the goal is to get a promotion, you can imagine yourself in the new office, hear the sounds of work, feel the satisfaction of recognition, and perceive the positive energy surrounding success. Visualization helps to program the brain for success, creating a clear mental image that can influence daily actions and decisions.

Another effective strategy is the use of positive affirmations. Affirmations are short, powerful statements that reflect your desires and positive beliefs. Regularly repeating affirmations such as "I am capable and deserve success" or "I attract abundance and opportunities into my life" can help reframe thinking, replacing doubts and fears with confidence and optimism. Affirmations can be repeated during meditation, written in a journal, or even visualized on post-its in strategic locations to constantly remind you of them.

Gratitude is another powerful tool in the law of attraction. Keeping a gratitude journal, where you note at least three things you are grateful for each day, can transform your perspective. Focusing on the blessings present in your life elevates your energetic vibration, attracting further reasons for gratitude. Gratitude not only improves mood but also creates positive energy that resonates with the universe, facilitating the attraction of positive experiences.

Furthermore, it is essential to act with intention. The law of attraction is not only about positive thinking but also about conscious action. Setting clear goals and breaking them down into concrete and manageable steps allows you to move determinedly towards your desires. Every small action taken with intention and awareness strengthens the connection between thought and manifestation, demonstrating commitment and dedication.

The surrounding environment also plays a crucial role. Creating a physical space that reflects your goals and desires can reinforce the practice of the law of attraction. For example, if you want to attract professional success, it is helpful to keep your workspace tidy and decorated with elements that inspire and motivate, such as positive quotes, images of achieved goals, and objects that evoke success.

Finally, surrounding yourself with positive and supportive people can make a big difference. Relationships deeply influence our emotional and mental state. Being around people who encourage, inspire, and share a positive mindset helps maintain a high energetic vibration and strengthens confidence in your dreams and goals.

By incorporating these practical strategies into daily life, it is possible to effectively apply the law of attraction, creating a more fulfilling life aligned with your deepest desires. These tools not only facilitate the achievement of your goals but also promote a sense of personal empowerment, demonstrating that everyone has the power to shape their reality through conscious thoughts, emotions, and actions.

Chapter 6

The Entanglement of the Mind

Definition of Entanglement and Its Application to the Human Mind

Quantum entanglement is one of the most fascinating and mysterious phenomena of modern physics, challenging our deepest intuitions about the nature of reality. Simply put, entanglement describes a situation where two or more particles become inextricably linked, to the point that the state of one particle is instantly correlated with the state of the other, regardless of the distance between them. This means that a change in the state of one particle causes an instant change in the state of the entangled particle, even if they are light-years apart.

This phenomenon, which Albert Einstein called "spooky action at a distance," seems to defy our traditional understanding of cause and effect and suggests the existence of deep, invisible connections that transcend space and time. But how can we apply this concept to the functioning of the human mind?

The idea of applying entanglement to the human mind emerges from interdisciplinary research that seeks to merge quantum physics, neuroscience, and psychology. Some theorists suggest that, at a fundamental level, our minds might be connected in a way similar to entangled particles, creating a network of interconnections that transcend our ordinary understanding of communication and mutual influence.

One of the most fascinating applications of this idea is the concept of "mental entanglement," which proposes that thoughts, emotions, and intentions can create invisible bonds between people. For example, telepathic intuition, where one person seems to perceive the thoughts or feelings of another without direct sensory communication, could be explained through a type of mental entanglement. This deep connection might allow for immediate and non-local communication, similar to what is observed between entangled particles.

Moreover, mental entanglement could explain phenomena like synchronicity, where seemingly unrelated events occur in a meaningful and unexpected way. Carl Jung, the famous Swiss psychologist, coined the term "synchronicity" to describe these meaningful coincidences that seem to connect minds and events in ways that defy traditional causality. If human minds are entangled, synchronicity could be a manifestation of these deep connections influencing multiple levels of reality simultaneously.

The implications of this concept are profound for understanding human relationships. Strong emotions and shared experiences could create entangled bonds between people, enhancing the sense of empathy and connection. This could explain why people who are very close, such as family members or close friends, often seem to "feel" when something happens to the other, even over great distances.

Studies on near-death experiences and out-of-body experiences suggest further possibilities for mental entanglement. People who have undergone such experiences often report feelings of universal connection and unity with all things, as if they were part of a larger network of consciousness. This could be seen as an indication that individual consciousness can interact with a quantum dimension of universal connection.

While the idea of mental entanglement is still speculative and requires further scientific research to be validated, it offers a fascinating perspective on how our minds might be connected at a deep and invisible level. If these connections truly exist, they could have significant implications for our understanding of consciousness, relationships, and the nature of reality itself.

Applying quantum entanglement to the human mind invites us to explore new horizons and consider the possibility that we are all part of a network of invisible connections that transcend space and time. This perspective not only enriches our scientific understanding but can also inspire a deeper sense of unity and interconnectedness among all living beings.

Studies and Research on Distant Mental Connections

Distant mental connections have fascinated scientists and researchers for decades, pushing the boundaries of our understanding of the mind and consciousness. Studies and research in this field seek to explore phenomena such as telepathy, synchronicity, and intuition, attempting to uncover the mechanisms that might allow two minds to connect without direct physical interaction.

One of the pioneers in studying distant mental connections was J.B. Rhine, a parapsychologist who conducted experiments on telepathy and other forms of extrasensory perception (ESP) at Duke University in the 1930s. Rhine used special cards, known as Zener cards, to test participants' ability to mentally transmit and receive information. Although Rhine's results were controversial and raised methodological criticisms, his studies paved the way for further research in the field of parapsychology.

In the 1970s, the Stargate Project, sponsored by the CIA and conducted at SRI International, explored remote viewing, a form of extrasensory perception in which participants attempted to describe distant objects or events. Participants, including the famous psychic Ingo Swann, reported remarkable successes, with detailed descriptions of places and objects they could not see directly. Although the Stargate Project was closed in 1995, its results continue to generate interest and debate about the possibility and mechanisms of distant mental connections.

More recently, research on "mental entanglement" has gained attention. Physicist and researcher Dean Radin at the Institute of Noetic Sciences has conducted experiments suggesting a connection between the mind and the quantum world. In one study, Radin and his team examined whether the focused intention of an observer could influence the behavior of subatomic particles in a device called an interferometer. The results indicated that the mind might have a measurable effect on the physical world, supporting the idea of non-local connections between consciousness and matter.

Another relevant field of research is "biofield science," which explores the energetic interactions between living organisms. Studies conducted by Beverly Rubik and colleagues have investigated how the energy fields produced by the human body can influence other people and living systems. These studies use advanced techniques such as Kirlian photography and spectroscopy to measure changes in energy fields in response to mental intentions and distant interactions.

Collective intuition, a phenomenon where groups of people seem to simultaneously perceive a future event or impending crisis, is another example of distant mental connections. Researchers like Rupert Sheldrake have proposed theories such as the "morphic field" to explain these connections. According to Sheldrake, morphic fields are invisible organizational patterns that link living beings, allowing the transmission of information and influences across distances.

A landmark experiment in this context was conducted by the Global Consciousness Project (GCP), which monitored fluctuations in "global consciousness" using a network of random number generators (RNGs) positioned worldwide. The GCP detected significant correlations between major emotionally impactful global events, such as terrorist attacks and natural disasters, and deviations in RNG data. These results suggest that collective human consciousness might have a measurable influence on non-local physical systems.

While many of these studies remain controversial and not fully accepted by the mainstream scientific community, they open up new possibilities for understanding the nature of the mind and its potential invisible connections. The phenomena of distant mental connections invite us to explore beyond the known boundaries, suggesting that consciousness might be far more interconnected and influential than we currently understand. These studies continue to stimulate debate and scientific investigation, contributing to a broader and deeper view of human capabilities and the nature of reality.

The Role of Emotions and Relationships in Mental Entanglement

Emotions and human relationships play a crucial role in mental entanglement, a phenomenon suggesting the existence of deep and invisible connections between people's minds. These connections can manifest through intense feelings and shared experiences, creating bonds that transcend time and space. Exploring how emotions and relationships influence mental entanglement offers a richer and more complex understanding of the nature of human consciousness.

Emotions are powerful catalysts for mental connections. When we experience strong emotions, such as love, fear, or joy, we emit a kind of "vibration" that can influence those around us. This phenomenon is evident in intimate relationships, where one person's emotions can be clearly perceived by the other, even at a distance. For example, couples married for a long time often report feeling their partner's emotions even when they are apart, experiencing a sense of connection that goes beyond simple verbal or physical communication.

Intense emotions can also facilitate phenomena like telepathy or shared intuition. In situations of danger or stress, for example, people may develop an almost telepathic connection with their loved ones, instinctively perceiving when something is wrong. This type of connection is often reported between parents and children, where a parent can "sense" when their child is in trouble, even without obvious signals. These experiences suggest that emotions can serve as a bridge for deep and immediate mental connections.

Relationships, particularly those based on affection and intimacy, seem to amplify mental entanglement. Strong emotional bonds create fertile ground for non-verbal communication and intuitive perception. Close friends, romantic partners, and family members often develop a mutual understanding that goes beyond words, being able to perceive each other's thoughts and feelings with surprising accuracy. This deep connection is often described as "attunement" or a "heart connection," reflecting the energetic and vibrational nature of these relationships.

Science has begun to explore these emotional and relational connections through studies on bioenergetic fields and synchronicity. Research in the field of biofield science, for example, suggests that the energy fields produced by the human body can interact and influence each other. These energetic interactions might explain how emotions and intentions can be "transmitted" between people, creating a sense of connection and attunement.

Another interesting aspect of mental entanglement in relationships is the concept of "empathetic resonance." When two people are emotionally close, their brainwaves can synchronize, a phenomenon known as "neural synchronization." This empathetic resonance allows for intuitive communication and mutual understanding that surpasses traditional communication barriers. Neuroimaging studies have shown that brain areas associated with empathy and social understanding activate simultaneously in people who share a strong emotional bond.

Emotions also play a crucial role in strengthening the bonds created by mental entanglement. Shared experiences of joy, pain, adventure, or hardship create emotionally charged memories that consolidate these connections. Emotions act as a glue, keeping people's minds connected even when they are physically apart.

Meditation and other mindfulness practices can amplify the ability to perceive these emotional and mental connections. Through meditation, people can develop greater awareness of their emotional states and energetic vibrations, enhancing their ability to attune to others. These practices can strengthen existing connections and open new pathways for intuitive communication.

In summary, emotions and relationships are fundamental in mental entanglement, creating a fabric of invisible connections that bind us in profound and meaningful ways. These bonds, fueled by intense emotions and intimate relationships, offer a more complete and rich understanding of the nature of human consciousness and its potential connections. Exploring these phenomena not only enriches our scientific understanding but also promotes a sense of empathy and interconnectedness that can transform our lives and relationships.

Case Studies and Accounts of Telepathic Connections

Telepathic connections, often considered the realm of science fiction, have been the subject of numerous studies and stories suggesting the possibility of communication through the mind. Although telepathy is not widely accepted by the mainstream scientific community, there are many case studies and testimonials that offer fascinating insights into this phenomenon.

One of the most famous cases is that of the Houghton twins. John and Michael Houghton, identical twins, have been the subject of numerous studies for their ability to perceive each other's thoughts and emotions, even when separated by great distances. During one of the experiments conducted by parapsychologist Montague Ullman in the 1960s, one of the twins was subjected to visual and sensory stimuli, while the other, in another room, reported similar experiences and sensations. The synchronized reactions of the Houghton twins raised many questions about the possibility of a mental connection that transcends physical space.

Another interesting case involves a woman named Sarah and her mother, Janet. During a business trip abroad, Sarah had an overwhelming and sudden feeling that her mother was in danger. Worried, she immediately called home and discovered that Janet had just had a domestic accident, falling down the stairs. This example of spontaneous telepathy between mother and daughter is representative of many anecdotal testimonies suggesting the possibility of deep mental connections in emergency situations.

In the field of academic research, a notable study was conducted by Rupert Sheldrake, a British biologist and parapsychologist. Sheldrake conducted experiments on the "sense of being stared at" and telephone telepathy. In his telephone telepathy experiments, participants were asked to guess who among four possible callers was about to call them. The results showed that participants guessed correctly at a rate higher than chance, suggesting some form of telepathic connection. Although Sheldrake's results have been criticized for methodological issues, they continue to stimulate discussions and further research in the field.

Another engaging account of telepathy involves a married couple, Tom and Lisa. During a period of separation due to work, Lisa woke up suddenly one night with a feeling of distress and a strong desire to call Tom. When she managed to contact him, she discovered that Tom had just been in a car accident and was in the hospital. The telepathic connection between the two, who had had no immediate physical or verbal contact, suggests that deep emotional bonds may facilitate the transmission of thoughts and feelings over distance.

In 1971, parapsychologist Charles Tart conducted experiments with a well-known psychic, Ingo Swann, to explore telepathy and remote viewing. During one of the experiments, Swann was able to accurately describe objects hidden in a separate room without any visual or physical contact. Although Tart's experiments were met with skepticism, they represent significant attempts to explore and document telepathic phenomena under controlled conditions.

These case studies and accounts, although varied in context and methodology, offer a fascinating overview of the potential telepathic abilities of humans. The wealth of anecdotal testimonies and the results of experimental studies, despite the controversies, suggest that there may be an unexplored dimension of the mind that allows for deep and immediate connections. As science continues to investigate these phenomena, personal experiences and accounts of telepathic connections remain fertile ground for understanding the complexity and potential of human consciousness.

Techniques for Developing and Strengthening Mental Entanglement with Others

Developing and strengthening mental entanglement with others may seem like a mysterious skill, but there are techniques that can help create deeper and more meaningful connections with people. These practices are based on principles of awareness, empathy, and intention and can enhance our ability to perceive and influence the emotions and thoughts of others.

One of the most effective techniques is mindfulness meditation. Meditation not only helps to calm the mind and reduce stress but also increases our ability to perceive the emotional vibrations and non-verbal cues of those around us. By practicing mindfulness meditation, we learn to focus attention on the present moment, becoming more sensitive to subtle changes in the environment and people. This heightened awareness can facilitate the perception of mental connections and improve empathy.

Another powerful practice is creative visualization. During visualization, imagining scenarios in which you mentally connect with a loved one can strengthen that bond. For example, you can visualize a light or energy flowing between yourself and the other person, symbolizing the connection and mental affinity. Repeating this visualization regularly can intensify the sense of union and harmony with the other person.

Empathetic communication techniques are essential for developing mental entanglement. Active listening, which involves fully attending to what the other person is saying without judging or interrupting, creates an environment of trust and understanding. Mirroring the other person's emotions and words, showing that you deeply understand what has been said, can strengthen the emotional and mental connection. This practice of empathetic communication helps build mental bridges that facilitate mutual perception and influence.

Breathing synchronization is another useful technique. When two people breathe in sync, it creates a sense of harmony and connection. This practice can be particularly effective among partners or close friends. Sitting together and focusing on breathing, trying to breathe in sync, can create a feeling of deep unity and resonance. This exercise not only strengthens mental entanglement but also promotes relaxation and emotional cohesion.

Focused intention is a key principle for strengthening mental entanglement. Spending time each day sending positive and loving thoughts to a loved one can create and maintain a mental connection. For example, you can visualize the other person while mentally sending thoughts of gratitude, love, and support. This not only strengthens the emotional bond but can also positively influence the other person, even if they are not physically present.

Practices of mindful touch, such as hugging or massage, can also intensify mental connections. Touch creates a physical link that can amplify the feeling of energetic and mental connection. When hugging a loved one, focusing on the positive energy flowing between you can strengthen mental entanglement.

Group or collective meditation can be a powerful experience for developing mental entanglement with a group of people. Meditating together, focusing on a common intention, creates a synergy that can amplify mental connections among participants. This type of meditation can be particularly useful in group or community work contexts where a strong sense of unity and collaboration is essential.

Finally, it is important to cultivate an open and positive mindset. Limiting beliefs and negative thoughts can hinder mental connections. Maintaining an attitude of openness, curiosity, and acceptance facilitates the creation of deep and meaningful mental bonds.

Incorporating these techniques into daily life can help develop and strengthen mental entanglement with others, creating deeper and more enriching connections that transcend simple physical and verbal interactions. These mental bonds not only improve personal relationships but can also lead to greater understanding and collaboration, both on an individual and collective level.

Chapter 7

Superposition and Infinite Potential

Explanation of Quantum Superposition and Multiple Possibilities

Quantum superposition is one of the most fascinating and revolutionary concepts in modern physics, and it represents a key element for understanding the nature of multiple possibilities in the universe. This idea originates from quantum mechanics, the theory that describes the behavior of subatomic particles, and it deeply challenges our intuitions about reality.

In simple terms, quantum superposition suggests that a particle can simultaneously exist in multiple different states until it is observed. This concept was first introduced by Erwin Schrödinger in 1935 with his famous thought experiment known as Schrödinger's cat. In the experiment, a cat is placed inside a box with a device that has a 50% chance of killing it, based on the decay of a radioactive particle. According to quantum mechanics, as long as the box remains closed and no one observes the cat's state, it exists in a superposition of states, being both alive and dead at the same time. Only when the box is opened and the cat is observed does the wave function collapse into one of the two definite states: alive or dead.

This superposition of states is not limited to thought experiments but has been experimentally demonstrated in laboratories with particles such as electrons and photons. In one of the most well-known experiments, called the double-slit experiment, photons are fired through two slits and then detected on a screen. When unobserved, the photons create an interference pattern characteristic of wave behavior, indicating that each photon simultaneously passes through both slits. However, if one tries to observe which slit the photon goes through, the interference pattern disappears, and the photons behave like particles passing through a single slit.

This wave-particle duality and the ability to exist in multiple states simultaneously introduce the notion of multiple possibilities. Quantum mechanics tells us that, at the subatomic level, reality is not deterministic but probabilistic. Each particle is described by a wave function that represents a set of probabilities for all the possible states the particle can be in. This means that, until it is observed, the particle exists in a combination of all these possible states.

Quantum superposition has profound implications not only for physics but also for philosophy and our understanding of reality. It suggests that the universe is fundamentally indeterminate, and that our observation plays a crucial role in determining the reality we experience. This has led to philosophical interpretations such as the many-worlds interpretation proposed by Hugh Everett, which posits that every possible outcome of a quantum measurement is realized in a distinct parallel universe. In this view, every decision and event create a continuous branching of parallel universes, each with a different history.

Practically, quantum superposition is the foundation of emerging technologies such as quantum computing. Quantum computers exploit superposition to perform parallel calculations on an exponential scale, using qubits that can represent both 0 and 1 simultaneously. This promises to revolutionize fields such as cryptography, the simulation of complex molecular systems, and the solution of advanced mathematical problems.

Understanding quantum superposition offers us a new perspective on the nature of reality, inviting us to consider that the world we perceive is just one of many existing possibilities. Quantum mechanics, with its probabilistic description and superposition of states, challenges us to rethink our traditional conceptions of certainty and determinism, opening the door to a universe rich with unexplored possibilities.

How the Concept of Infinite Potential Applies to the Human Mind

The concept of infinite potential, derived from quantum superposition, finds a surprising application in the human mind, offering a fascinating perspective on our capacity for growth and transformation. Quantum superposition teaches us that particles can exist in multiple states simultaneously until they are observed, suggesting that the universe is a field of infinite possibilities. Applying this concept to the human mind, we can see our consciousness and potential as a vast space of possibilities waiting to be explored and realized.

The human mind, with its incredible capacity for thought, creativity, and adaptability, is a perfect example of infinite potential. Each thought, emotion, and decision represents a fork in our personal reality, a choice among multiple possibilities. This idea is well represented in the concept of neuroplasticity, which refers to the brain's ability to reorganize itself by forming new neural connections in response to learning, experience, and change. Neuroplasticity demonstrates that our brain is not static but dynamic and capable of continuous growth, much like particles in superposition that can manifest in different states.

One way infinite potential manifests in the human mind is through creativity. Creativity is the ability to generate new and original ideas, solutions, and approaches. When faced with a creative problem, our mind simultaneously explores a range of possibilities, combining and rearranging information in new and innovative ways. This mental exploration of multiple possibilities reflects the concept of quantum superposition, where each idea represents a potential reality that can be realized through action and intention.

Intuition is another example of how infinite potential applies to the human mind. Intuition is the ability to understand or know something immediately, without the need for conscious reasoning. It often emerges from an unconscious process that integrates and analyzes multiple pieces of information and experiences simultaneously. This intuitive process can be seen as a sort of mental superposition, where the mind simultaneously explores various possibilities and selects the one most suitable for the situation.

The infinite potential of the mind also manifests in our learning and adaptability capabilities. Faced with new challenges and environments, the human mind can quickly adapt, developing new skills and strategies. This continuous adaptation reflects the mind's ability to explore and realize a range of possibilities, maintaining the flexibility necessary to face uncertainty and change. The ability to learn and grow in response to new experiences is a testament to the infinite potential inherent in every individual.

Meditation and other mindfulness practices can amplify our ability to access this infinite potential. Meditation helps to calm the mind and create a space of quiet where the depths of consciousness can be explored. In this state of quiet, the mind is free to wander and explore possibilities that might otherwise be hidden by daily worries and distractions. This process of inner exploration can lead to profound insights and new realizations, manifesting the infinite potential of the mind.

Moreover, the concept of infinite potential applies to human relationships and our ability to connect with others. Each social interaction is an opportunity to explore new dynamics and create meaningful connections. Relationships based on empathy, understanding, and mutual respect can continuously evolve and deepen, offering infinite opportunities for mutual growth and enrichment.

In summary, the concept of infinite potential, derived from quantum superposition, finds a powerful application in the human mind. Our capacity to think, create, intuit, learn, and adapt reflects a field of infinite possibilities that we can explore and realize. Embracing this potential, we can transform our lives and experiences, tapping into the depths of our consciousness to manifest a rich and meaningful reality.

Examples of Creativity and Innovation Derived from the Quantum Mind

Creativity and innovation are often considered the driving forces behind human progress, fueled by a mind capable of exploring a field of infinite possibilities, much like the theory of the quantum mind suggests. This ability to think beyond conventional limits and see invisible connections between seemingly disparate ideas has led to revolutionary discoveries and inventions throughout history.

One emblematic example of creativity stemming from the quantum mind is the invention of Velcro. George de Mestral, a Swiss engineer, got the idea while walking in the woods and noticing how burdock burrs clung to his clothes and his dog's fur. Instead of seeing this as a mere annoyance, de Mestral explored the microscopic structure of the burrs and discovered the tiny hooks that allowed them to latch on tightly. This observation led him to develop Velcro, a fastening system that has revolutionized numerous sectors, from fashion to medical technology. De Mestral demonstrated a quantum mindset, seeing innovative possibilities where others saw only inconvenience.

Another extraordinary example is the discovery of penicillin by Alexander Fleming. Fleming was studying bacterial cultures when he noticed that one of his Petri dishes was contaminated with mold. Instead of discarding the dish, Fleming observed that the mold seemed to inhibit bacterial growth. This moment of insight led him to isolate penicillin, the first antibiotic, which has saved millions of lives. Fleming's ability to recognize the significance of an apparently insignificant event and see a positive potential in an anomalous situation reflects a quantum mindset of exploration and innovation.

In the field of technology, Steve Jobs is often cited as an example of a quantum mind. His vision for Apple was not merely to create electronic products but to transform the way people interact with technology. Jobs combined elements of design, functionality, and user experience in innovative ways, creating products that not only met consumer needs but anticipated them. The iPhone, for example, revolutionized the mobile phone industry by integrating functions that redefined the concept of the smartphone. Jobs showed an extraordinary ability to see possibilities that others did not, manifesting the infinite potential of the quantum mind through creativity and innovation.

The quantum mind also manifests in the field of art. Pablo Picasso, one of the greatest artists of the 20th century, revolutionized art with his Cubist style, which fragmented and recombined forms in new and unexpected ways. Picasso saw the world from multiple perspectives simultaneously, reflecting quantum superposition. This ability to see beyond conventional forms and explore new modes of visual representation had a lasting impact on modern art, opening up new avenues of creative expression.

In the scientific world, Albert Einstein's quantum mind led him to formulate the theory of relativity, which transformed our understanding of space and time. Einstein not only imagined complex concepts like the curvature of space-time but made them understandable through innovative thought experiments, such as the famous twin paradox. His ability to explore ideas outside conventional scientific paradigms opened new frontiers in physics and demonstrated the power of creativity and innovation derived from a quantum mind.

In summary, creativity and innovation derived from the quantum mind are evident in numerous historical and contemporary examples. These examples show how the ability to see beyond appearances, explore multiple possibilities, and combine ideas in new and unexpected ways can lead to revolutionary discoveries and inventions. The quantum mind, with its infinite potential, invites us to think beyond conventional boundaries and imagine a world of limitless possibilities.

Techniques for Exploring and Realizing Multiple Potentials in Your Life

Exploring and realizing multiple potentials in your life is a fascinating adventure that requires an open mind, creativity, and a strategic approach. Here are some effective techniques to help unlock and manifest the many possibilities within us.

A powerful tool for exploring your potential is creative visualization. This practice involves vividly and detailedly imagining your goals as if they have already been achieved. Visualization helps create a clear mental image of what you want to achieve, stimulating the brain to recognize and seize opportunities. For example, imagining success in a new career can generate the courage and motivation needed to pursue it. Engaging all senses during visualization makes the experience more realistic and strengthens the connection between thought and action.

Meditation is another fundamental technique for accessing your potential. Regular meditation calms the mind and promotes awareness, allowing you to identify and overcome limiting thoughts. During meditation, you can focus your attention on desired goals, letting intuition emerge and offering new perspectives. Meditation also helps develop the ability to stay focused and resilient in the face of challenges, facilitating the path towards achieving your goals.

Adopting a growth mindset is essential for exploring and realizing multiple potentials. This approach, conceptualized by Carol Dweck, involves the belief that abilities and skills can be developed through effort and perseverance. Embracing a growth mindset means seeing challenges as learning opportunities and considering failure as part of the growth process. This positive attitude encourages the adoption of new experiences and the overcoming of self-imposed limits, opening the way to infinite possibilities.

Journaling is another effective tool for exploring your potential. Regularly writing down your thoughts, emotions, and goals helps clarify ideas and identify limiting thought patterns. Through journaling, you can explore different options and scenarios, assess progress, and reflect on experiences. This practice of self-reflection facilitates the identification of new goals and strategies, allowing you to chart a clear path towards realizing your dreams.

Experimenting and stepping out of your comfort zone are crucial for discovering new possibilities. Trying new activities, learning new skills, and facing unknown challenges can reveal hidden talents and unexpected passions. Experimentation requires courage and an open mind, but each step into the unknown enriches your life and expands the field of possibilities. Every new experience offers valuable lessons and growth opportunities, making the journey towards realizing your potential an ongoing adventure.

Social networks play a significant role in facilitating the exploration and realization of your potentials. Connecting with people who share similar interests or have diverse experiences can offer new perspectives and inspire innovative ideas. Meaningful relationships provide emotional and practical support, and collaborations can lead to results that would be difficult to achieve alone. Joining interest groups, networking events, and online communities can expand your horizons and open doors to new opportunities.

Finally, setting clear goals and breaking them down into concrete steps is essential for transforming multiple potentials into reality. Establishing specific, measurable, achievable, relevant, and time-bound (SMART) goals helps maintain focus and monitor progress. Each small step towards the final goal represents a success that strengthens motivation and self-confidence. This strategic approach allows you to tackle the journey towards realizing your dreams with determination and clarity.

In summary, exploring and realizing multiple potentials in your life requires a combination of creative visualization, meditation, growth mindset, journaling, experimentation, social networks, and strategic planning. These techniques help uncover new possibilities and transform dreams into concrete realities, allowing you to live a richer and more fulfilling life. By embracing these practices, you can tap into the infinite potential within you and manifest a reality aligned with your deepest aspirations and goals.

Philosophical and Spiritual Implications of Infinite Potential

The philosophical and spiritual implications of the concept of infinite potential are profound and transformative, touching the very roots of our understanding of reality, the self, and our role in the universe. This concept, derived from quantum superposition and the idea that every moment contains a myriad of possibilities, invites a broader reflection on the meaning of life and consciousness.

Philosophically, infinite potential pushes us to reconsider the concept of determinism. Quantum mechanics suggests that the universe is not predetermined but rather a field of possibilities that realize through the choices and observations of individuals. This view opens the door to a new level of personal freedom and responsibility. If every choice we make can significantly influence the course of our lives, then every moment becomes an opportunity to create the reality we desire. This idea resonates with existential philosophies that emphasize the importance of individual choices and the ability to create meaning in one's life.

Spiritually, the concept of infinite potential is closely tied to the idea that every human being possesses a divine spark or a connection to a universal field of consciousness. Many spiritual traditions teach that the human soul or spirit is inherently connected to a higher power or a source of infinite wisdom. This infinite potential can be seen as a reflection of our connection to this higher dimension. Meditation, prayer, and other spiritual practices are often used to access this potential, revealing deep insights and guiding life's path toward greater harmony and fulfillment.

The notion of infinite potential also challenges our understanding of time. Quantum physics and many spiritual traditions suggest that time is not linear but rather a series of present moments containing all possible futures. This view invites us to live more fully in the present, recognizing that each moment is laden with potential. Practices of mindfulness and presence help us tune into this potential, allowing us to seize opportunities that might otherwise elude us.

Another important philosophical implication concerns the interconnection of all things. Infinite potential suggests that we are all part of a vast fabric of existence, where every action and every thought influence the whole. This idea is reflected in the concept of karma in Eastern philosophies, which holds that our actions create waves of cause and effect that reverberate through time and space. Recognizing our interconnectedness with all living beings can inspire a sense of responsibility and compassion, promoting actions that contribute to the collective well-being.

From a spiritual perspective, infinite potential can be seen as an invitation to rediscover our true selves and live in harmony with our highest purpose. Many spiritual teachings suggest that we are here to realize our highest potential, to express our unique creativity, and to contribute positively to the world. This path of personal realization is often described as a journey of awakening, where we become aware of our innate capacities and learn to live in alignment with our true purpose.

Finally, the concept of infinite potential can lead to greater open-mindedness and a willingness to explore new horizons. If every situation contains an infinity of possibilities, then an attitude of curiosity and inquiry becomes a philosophy of life. This approach encourages us to keep learning, growing, and evolving, recognizing that our potential is limited only by our beliefs and imagination.

In conclusion, the philosophical and spiritual implications of infinite potential are vast and profound, inviting us to explore new dimensions of consciousness and live a life rich with meaning, connection, and possibility. This vision inspires us to see every moment as an opportunity to create, grow, and contribute to the grand tapestry of existence.

Chapter 8

The Role of the Observer

The Concept of the Observer in Quantum Physics and Psychology

The concept of the observer occupies a central role in both quantum physics and psychology, revealing profound parallels between these two seemingly disparate disciplines. In both fields, the act of observation is not a passive process but a dynamic interaction that can influence the observed system and determine the final outcomes. This principle underscores the importance of awareness and perception, demonstrating how our experience of reality is intimately linked to how we observe it.

In quantum physics, the observer plays a crucial role through the so-called "observer effect." This phenomenon has been highlighted in double-slit experiments, where particles like photons and electrons behave differently depending on whether they are observed or not. When not observed, the particles simultaneously pass through both slits, creating an interference pattern characteristic of waves. However, when a measuring device is positioned to determine which slit the particle passes through, the interference pattern disappears, and the particles behave like discrete objects. This suggests that the act of observing alters the state of the particle, collapsing the wave function into a single reality.

This concept has profound philosophical implications. It suggests that reality at the quantum level is not determined until it is observed, making the observer an integral part of the reality-creation process. In other words, our perception can influence and define the quantum world, raising fundamental questions about the nature of reality and the role of consciousness in the universe.

Similarly, in psychology, the role of the observer is equally significant. Cognitive psychology, in particular, explores how our perceptions and interpretations of the world influence our emotions and behaviors. According to cognitive theory, it is not the event itself that determines our emotional state but rather how we interpret it. For instance, two people may react very differently to the same situation, depending on their beliefs, past experiences, and expectations. This reflects the principle that our observation and interpretation of reality are essential in determining our subjective experience.

Another significant example of the observer's role in psychology is the phenomenon of "confirmation bias." This cognitive bias occurs when people seek, interpret, and remember information in a way that confirms their preexisting beliefs. This process of selective observation profoundly influences how we perceive the world, reinforcing our convictions and shaping our personal reality.

The concept of the observer is also central to mindfulness and awareness practices. Mindfulness, a practice derived from Eastern meditative traditions, emphasizes the importance of observing one's thoughts and emotions without judgment. This form of mindful observation allows for greater self-understanding and acceptance, promoting mental well-being. Here, the internal observer acts as a neutral witness, facilitating a perspective shift that can transform personal experience.

The intersections between quantum physics and psychology on the role of the observer offer a fascinating view of the nature of reality. In both fields, observation is not merely a passive act of recording but an active interaction that influences what is being observed. This suggests that our perception and awareness play a crucial role in shaping our experience of the world.

This connection between physics and psychology invites reflection on the power of consciousness and the influence it exerts on reality. Recognizing the power of the observer encourages us to develop greater awareness of our thoughts and perceptions, promoting a more responsible and creative approach to our daily lives. Ultimately, the concept of the observer reminds us that we are co-creators of our reality, with the ability to influence both the internal and external worlds through the way we choose to see and interact with them.

How Observation Affects Reality and Personal Events

The idea that observation can influence reality and personal events is one of the most fascinating and provocative concepts in both quantum physics and psychology. This notion challenges the traditional view of the world as a collection of objective events, suggesting instead that our perception and awareness can actively shape the reality we experience.

In quantum physics, the observer effect has been widely demonstrated through various experiments. One of the most well-known is the double-slit experiment, which shows how subatomic particles behave differently depending on whether they are observed or not. When not observed, the particles exhibit wave-like behavior, passing through both slits simultaneously and creating an interference pattern. However, when an observer measures which slit the particle passes through, the behavior of the particles changes, manifesting as discrete particles that pass through only one slit. This experiment demonstrates that the act of observation alters the state of the particles, suggesting that observation itself is an integral part of physical reality.

This principle finds an echo in psychology, where observation and interpretation play a crucial role in shaping our personal experience. According to cognitive theory, our perception of events is mediated by our beliefs, expectations, and interpretations. For example, two people witnessing the same event may have very different emotional reactions depending on how they interpret it. If one person sees a change as an opportunity, they may feel excitement and optimism, while another who perceives it as a threat may feel fear and anxiety. This shows that our observation and interpretation of events directly influence our emotional and behavioral experience.

Another relevant example is the phenomenon of "confirmation bias." This cognitive bias occurs when people tend to seek, interpret, and remember information that confirms their preexisting beliefs. For instance, a person who believes they are not appreciated at work will more easily notice signals that confirm this belief, while ignoring or minimizing evidence to the contrary. This process of selective observation not only reinforces existing beliefs but also shapes perceived reality, creating a self-perpetuating cycle of confirmation.

Mindful observation also plays a fundamental role in mindfulness and meditation practices. Mindfulness teaches observing one's thoughts and emotions without judgment, promoting greater awareness and acceptance of the present moment. This form of mindful observation can transform our experience, helping us respond more balanced and less reactively to life's challenges. When we consciously observe our reactions, we can choose to change our responses, positively influencing our personal reality.

Another way observation influences reality is through focused intention. Research has shown that intentionally focusing thoughts on specific goals can influence outcomes. This is the principle behind creative visualization techniques, where one vividly imagines achieving a desired goal. Focused intention can help create a reality where such goals become more attainable, as observation and intention shape daily actions and decisions towards their realization.

In summary, observation profoundly affects reality and personal events on both a quantum and psychological level. Quantum physics shows us that the act of observing can alter the state of particles, suggesting that reality is partly determined by our interaction with it. Similarly, psychology teaches us that our perception and interpretation of events shape our experience of the world, influencing our emotions and behaviors. Understanding the power of observation invites us to become conscious and intentional observers of our lives, recognizing that we can actively influence reality through our perception and awareness.

Studies and Research on the Power of Attention and Intention

The power of attention and intention has garnered interest from scientists and researchers across various fields, including psychology, quantum physics, and medicine. Studies on these phenomena suggest that our mind has a profound and measurable influence on reality and personal events.

One of the pioneers in the study of attention was William James, often considered the father of American psychology. James emphasized that attention is a limited and precious resource capable of shaping our experience of the world. According to him, what we choose to focus our attention on determines our subjective reality. This insight inspired decades of research into how attention can influence our perceptions and actions.

A contemporary example of research on attention is the "invisible gorilla" experiment conducted by Christopher Chabris and Daniel Simons. In this study, participants were asked to count the number of times a ball was passed between players while a man in a gorilla costume walked through the scene. Surprisingly, many participants did not notice the gorilla, demonstrating how focused attention can exclude significant elements of the environment. This experiment illustrates the power of attention in shaping our perception of reality, highlighting its selective and limited nature.

Intention, on the other hand, has been extensively studied in more esoteric and innovative contexts. Dean Radin, a researcher at the Institute of Noetic Sciences, has explored the power of human intention through controlled experiments. In a famous study, Radin examined whether focused intention could influence the behavior of subatomic particles in a quantum interferometer. The results suggested that human intentions could indeed have a measurable effect on the physical system, supporting the idea that the mind can interact with matter at a fundamental level.

Research on the power of intention also extends to medicine. The study of placebo effects is a clear example of how beliefs and expectations can influence clinical outcomes. Patients who believe they are receiving an effective treatment often experience significant improvements in symptoms, even if the treatment is inert. This phenomenon demonstrates that positive expectations and the intention to heal can stimulate real physiological processes in the body.

Another field that has explored intention is meditation and energy healing practices. Herbert Benson, a Harvard physician, studied the effects of meditation on health and found that regular practice can reduce stress, lower blood pressure, and improve immune function. These benefits are partly attributed to focused intention and awareness, which promote a state of deep relaxation and regeneration.

Lynn McTaggart, an author and researcher, has also explored the power of intention through "The Intention Experiment." McTaggart conducted global experiments where groups of people focused positive intentions on a specific goal, such as plant growth or reducing violence in a community. The results of these experiments showed significant effects, suggesting that collective intention can influence physical and social events.

Neuroplasticity offers another perspective on the power of attention and intention. Neuroscience studies have shown that the brain is highly plastic and can reorganize itself in response to thoughts, experiences, and intentional practices. Mindfulness meditation, for example, has been associated with structural changes in the brain, such as increased gray matter density in areas related to awareness and emotional regulation.

In summary, studies on the power of attention and intention reveal a deep connection between the mind and reality. From psychology to quantum physics, and from medicine to neuroscience, research suggests that our minds are not mere passive observers but active participants in the creation of our experience. These findings invite us to consider more carefully how we use our awareness and intention to shape the world around us, offering new possibilities for personal and collective well-being.

Techniques to Become a Mindful and Intentional Observer

Becoming a mindful and intentional observer requires practice and dedication, but the benefits of this transformation can be profoundly enriching. Awareness and intentionality in observation not only improve the quality of our daily lives but also enable us to positively influence our reality. Here are some effective techniques to develop these skills.

Mindfulness meditation is one of the most powerful techniques for cultivating mindful observation. The practice of mindfulness involves bringing attention to the present moment in a non-judgmental way. Sitting quietly, focusing on the breath, and observing thoughts and emotions as they arise without attachment helps develop greater self-awareness. Over time, this practice teaches us to observe our thoughts and reactions with detachment, recognizing them as transient and not definitive. This state of mindful observation allows us to respond to situations with greater calm and clarity.

Another effective technique is creative visualization. This practice involves vividly imagining positive and desired scenarios, engaging all senses to make the experience as realistic as possible. Visualizing oneself achieving specific goals helps program the brain to recognize and seize opportunities that lead to these outcomes. Visualization not only boosts confidence and motivation but also reinforces intention, facilitating the transition from passive observation to conscious action.

Keeping a journal is another powerful tool for becoming a mindful and intentional observer. Regularly writing about thoughts, emotions, and goals helps clarify ideas and reflect on experiences. This practice of self-reflection allows for the identification of limiting thought patterns and the exploration of new perspectives. Journaling facilitates awareness of mental processes and reactions, promoting greater control over daily actions and decisions.

Learning to practice active listening is another fundamental technique. Active listening involves giving full attention to the speaker, striving to understand their point of view without interrupting or judging. This form of listening not only improves interpersonal relationships but also develops the ability to observe and understand others better. Active listening promotes empathy and connection, allowing us to become more mindful observers of social dynamics and others' emotions.

Mindful breathing is a simple yet effective technique for anchoring attention to the present moment. Focusing on the rhythm of the breath, feeling the air enter and exit the lungs, helps calm the mind and reduce stress. Mindful breathing can be practiced at any time of the day, offering a quick way to return to a state of presence and awareness. This technique strengthens the ability to observe real-time reactions, allowing for more deliberate and intentional responses.

Finally, it is important to cultivate an attitude of gratitude. Taking time to reflect on what we are grateful for each day helps focus attention on the positive aspects of life. Gratitude increases emotional well-being and promotes a more optimistic and open view of the world. Being thankful for the small and large things in life makes us more aware of the blessings we receive, enhancing our ability to observe and appreciate reality with greater depth and intentionality.

Becoming a mindful and intentional observer is an ongoing journey that requires practice and commitment. By using these techniques, we can develop greater self-awareness and a deeper understanding of the world around us, improving our ability to positively influence our reality. This transformation not only enriches our personal experience but also enables us to live more authentically and meaningfully, in harmony with our deepest values and goals.

Practical Examples of How Mindful Observation Can Transform Reality

Mindful observation has the power to transform reality in profound and meaningful ways, offering a new perspective on life and everyday experiences. Here are some practical examples of how this practice can positively influence various aspects of our existence.

Consider a manager who oversees a diverse team with different personalities and work styles. Through mindful observation, this manager can develop a deeper understanding of team dynamics. Instead of reacting impulsively to tensions or conflicts, the manager practices active listening and carefully observes interactions among team members. This awareness helps identify underlying causes of problems and address them with empathy and strategy. The result is a more harmonious work environment where employees feel heard and valued, boosting team productivity and morale.

In personal life, mindful observation can transform interpersonal relationships. Take the example of a couple experiencing communication difficulties. By using techniques of mindful observation, such as mindfulness and active listening, each partner can learn to better recognize and understand their own feelings and those of the other. This leads to more open and honest communication, reducing misunderstandings and strengthening the emotional bond. When both partners commit to being present and aware in their interactions, the relationship can evolve in a more positive and constructive direction.

Another example of how mindful observation can transform reality is in the field of health and well-being. A person suffering from chronic stress can greatly benefit from mindfulness practice. By learning to observe their thoughts and physical sensations without judgment, this person can develop greater awareness of stress triggers and automatic reactions. Over time, this practice allows for more calm and clear responses to stressful situations, reducing the negative impact of stress on mental and physical health.

Mindfulness helps create an inner space of tranquility, improving the quality of life and promoting a sense of balance and well-being.

In the creative sphere, mindful observation can stimulate innovation and inspiration. An artist, for example, can use mindfulness to explore new ways of seeing and interpreting the world. By consciously observing their own emotions and reactions, the artist can access a deeper level of creativity and authenticity. This practice can lead to artworks that reflect a deeper and more sincere understanding of the human condition, enriching both the artist and the audience.

In the context of learning and personal growth, mindful observation can make a significant difference. A student practicing mindfulness can improve their concentration and learning ability. Being aware of distracting thoughts and emotions while studying allows for refocusing on the current task, increasing learning effectiveness. This awareness can also help develop strategies to manage exam anxiety and improve overall academic performance.

Finally, mindful observation can transform the relationship with oneself. Practices like journaling and meditation help develop greater awareness of one's thoughts, emotions, and behaviors. This self-observation can lead to a deeper understanding of oneself, promoting self-acceptance and self-love. By recognizing and embracing one's authenticity, one can live a more fulfilling and authentic life in harmony with their values and goals.

In conclusion, mindful observation has the power to transform various aspects of our reality, from interpersonal relationships to mental health, from creativity to learning. This practice invites us to be present and intentional in our daily experiences, promoting a richer and more meaningful life.

Chapter 9

Neuroscience and Meditation

Effects of Meditation on the Brain: The Neuroscience of Mindfulness

Meditation, particularly mindfulness, has gained increasing attention not only for its psychological benefits but also for its tangible effects on the brain. The neuroscience of mindfulness explores how meditative practice influences brain structure and function, providing a scientific understanding of how these techniques can enhance overall well-being.

One of the most well-known effects of meditation on the brain is neuroplasticity, the brain's ability to reorganize itself by forming new neural connections. Functional magnetic resonance imaging (fMRI) studies have shown that meditation can increase the density of gray matter in key areas of the brain. For example, the prefrontal cortex, associated with planning, decision-making, and self-control, shows increased gray matter density in meditation practitioners. This suggests that meditation can improve executive functions and emotional regulation.

Another brain area influenced by meditation is the hippocampus, involved in memory and learning. Regular mindfulness practice has been associated with increased hippocampal volume, which can help enhance memory and cognitive abilities. Additionally, the hippocampus is also linked to stress regulation. The increased volume of the hippocampus in meditators may explain why mindfulness is effective in reducing symptoms of anxiety and depression.

Meditation also has a significant impact on the amygdala, a brain structure involved in emotional responses and fear regulation. Studies have shown that meditation can reduce the volume of the amygdala, suggesting a decrease in stress and fear responses. This is particularly relevant for individuals suffering from anxiety disorders or post-traumatic stress disorder, as reducing amygdala activity can lead to greater emotional resilience and better management of negative emotions.

Another important effect of meditation involves the brain's functional connectivity, which is how different regions of the brain communicate with each other. Mindfulness practice has been associated with increased connectivity between the prefrontal cortex and the amygdala, improving the ability to regulate emotional responses. Additionally, meditation increases connectivity between the default mode network (DMN) and other brain regions, contributing to greater self-awareness and reduced mental rumination. The DMN is a brain network active when the mind is at rest and not focused on external tasks; greater connectivity in this network can lead to enhanced present-moment awareness and reduced automatic negative thinking.

Meditation not only modifies brain structure but also influences brain function. Electroencephalographic (EEG) studies have revealed that meditation can increase alpha waves, which are associated with a state of relaxation and reduced anxiety. Moreover, mindfulness practice is associated with an increase in gamma waves, which are linked to heightened attention and awareness. These changes in brain waves suggest that meditation can enhance concentration and moment-to-moment awareness.

Finally, meditation can influence the production of neurotransmitters such as serotonin and dopamine, which play crucial roles in mood regulation and overall well-being. The increase in these neurotransmitters may explain why meditation is often associated with improved mood and reduced symptoms of depression.

In summary, the neuroscience of mindfulness provides clear evidence of the profound effects of meditation on the brain. Regular meditation practice can lead to structural and functional changes that enhance emotional regulation, memory, attention, and overall well-being. These benefits not only enrich daily life but also offer effective tools for addressing psychological challenges and improving quality of life.

Meditation Techniques and Their Impact on the Mind and Perception

Meditation techniques are diverse and varied, each with a unique impact on the mind and perception. Exploring these techniques helps us understand how different meditative approaches can transform our mental state and experience of the world.

One of the most widespread techniques is mindfulness meditation, which focuses on bringing attention to the present moment in a non-judgmental way. This practice involves observing thoughts, emotions, and bodily sensations as they arise, without attempting to change or avoid them. Mindfulness helps develop greater self-awareness and acceptance, reducing stress and anxiety. Over time, practicing mindfulness can improve emotional regulation and increase mental resilience, leading to greater inner calm and a more balanced perception of reality.

Another widely practiced technique is Transcendental Meditation (TM). This method involves the use of a mantra, a word or phrase repeated silently, to help the mind reach a state of deep rest and transcendent awareness. TM is known for its ability to reduce stress and promote a sense of inner peace. Studies have shown that this technique can lower blood pressure, improve cardiac function, and enhance psychological well-being. The repetition of the mantra helps to calm incessant thoughts, allowing the mind to transcend the normal waking state and experience a deeper level of consciousness.

Zen meditation, or Zazen, is another form of meditation that has a significant impact on the mind and perception. Practiced mainly in Japanese Buddhist traditions, Zen meditation focuses on posture, breathing, and contemplation. Practitioners sit in a specific position, often cross-legged, and concentrate on their breathing, allowing thoughts to arise and dissipate without attachment. Zen meditation promotes mental calmness, concentration, and insight. Over time, this practice can lead to greater mental clarity and a profound understanding of one's inner nature.

Vipassana meditation, which means "insight" or "clear seeing," is a technique that focuses on observing bodily sensations and awareness of one's moment-to-moment experience. This practice, rooted in ancient Buddhist tradition, teaches the observation of internal and external phenomena with equanimity, recognizing the impermanence of all experiences. Vipassana meditation can help free oneself from mental conditioning and reactive habits, leading to greater inner freedom and a clearer, more authentic perception of reality.

Guided meditation is another popular technique, especially for beginners. In this practice, an instructor guides meditators through an imaginative journey or a mindfulness exercise. Guided meditation can vary widely, including visualizations of relaxing scenarios, inner explorations, or focusing on specific wellness goals. This technique can help reduce stress, improve concentration, and promote a sense of overall well-being. The vocal guidance helps maintain focused attention and develop a deeper, more structured meditative practice.

Lastly, walking meditation combines physical movement with meditative awareness. During walking meditation, attention is focused on the movements of the body and the physical sensations while walking slowly and deliberately. This practice helps ground oneself in the present moment and develop greater awareness of the body and the surrounding environment. Walking meditation can be particularly useful for those who find it challenging to sit still for long periods, offering a dynamic alternative to traditional meditation.

In summary, meditation techniques vary widely, but they all share the goal of enhancing awareness, mental calmness, and perception. Each technique offers unique benefits and can be tailored to individual needs, allowing anyone to explore and develop a meditative practice that enriches daily life and promotes overall well-being.

How Meditation Can Improve the Mind-Body Connection

Meditation is an ancient practice that has shown profound effects on the mind-body connection. Rooted in many cultural and spiritual traditions, it is gaining increasing attention in the Western world for its scientifically proven benefits. Meditation not only enhances mental health but also has a significant impact on physical well-being, promoting a harmonious connection between mind and body.

One of the primary ways meditation improves the mind-body connection is by reducing stress. Chronic stress is known to have detrimental effects on both the mind and body, contributing to a wide range of health issues such as anxiety, depression, heart disease, and digestive problems. Meditation reduces levels of cortisol, the stress hormone, helping to calm the nervous system. When the body is less stressed, physiological functions improve, promoting a general sense of well-being. This stress reduction creates a virtuous cycle where a calmer mind contributes to a healthier body and vice versa.

Meditation also enhances body awareness, which is fundamental for improving the mind-body connection. Practices like mindfulness teach individuals to pay attention to physical sensations, such as breathing, muscle tension, and heartbeat. This awareness helps recognize and address signs of discomfort or stress before they become more serious problems. For example, during a meditation session, one might notice tension in the neck or shoulders, and through awareness and intentional relaxation, alleviate this tension. This process of listening and responding to bodily signals improves communication between mind and body, promoting harmonious balance.

Another crucial aspect of meditation is mindful breathing. Many meditation techniques focus on the breath, which not only calms the mind but also has direct physiological effects. Slow, deep breathing activates the parasympathetic nervous system, responsible for rest and digestion, counteracting the activation of the sympathetic nervous system associated with the fight-or-flight response. This balance between the two nervous systems helps stabilize heart rate, improve digestion, and promote healing. Practicing mindful breathing during meditation teaches how to use the breath as a tool to maintain calm and control, even in stressful daily situations.

Meditation can also improve sleep quality, which is essential for a good mind-body connection. Sleep quality is closely linked to mental and physical health. Regular meditation can help calm the mind before sleep, reducing anxiety and intrusive thoughts that can interfere with sleep. Quality sleep allows the body to regenerate and the mind to rest, creating a solid foundation to face daily challenges with more energy and resilience.

Moreover, meditation has been shown to have positive effects on the immune system. Studies have shown that regular meditation practice can increase the activity of natural killer cells, which are crucial in defending the body against infections and diseases. A strong immune system is a clear indicator of a good mind-body connection, where a calm and focused mind contributes to optimal physical health.

Finally, meditation promotes greater self-acceptance and a positive perception of one's body. This is particularly important in a culture that often promotes unrealistic ideals of beauty and perfection. Through meditation, one develops greater compassion towards oneself, accepting the body as it is and recognizing its wisdom and healing capabilities. This self-acceptance and self-love improve self-esteem and promote a deeper and more loving connection between mind and body.

In summary, meditation is a powerful practice that strengthens the mind-body connection through stress reduction, body awareness, mindful breathing, improved sleep quality, enhanced immune function, and the promotion of self-acceptance. These combined benefits not only improve mental and physical well-being but also create a more harmonious and balanced life.

Scientific Studies on the Mental Health Benefits of Meditation

In recent decades, meditation has become the subject of numerous scientific studies, which have documented its significant benefits for mental health. These research efforts have provided compelling evidence that meditative practice can profoundly transform our psychological well-being, offering a range of advantages from stress reduction to increased emotional resilience.

One of the most influential studies in the field of meditation was conducted by Jon Kabat-Zinn, founder of the Mindfulness-Based Stress Reduction (MBSR) program. His work demonstrated that mindfulness can significantly reduce stress levels and improve quality of life. Participants in the MBSR program, which includes meditation practices, showed marked reductions in symptoms of anxiety and depression, along with improvements in awareness and general well-being. This pioneering study paved the way for further research on the benefits of meditation for mental health.

Meditation has also been extensively studied for its effect on depression. A meta-analysis published in JAMA Internal Medicine examined 47 clinical trials involving over 3,500 participants, finding that mindfulness meditation is as effective as antidepressants in treating mild to moderate depression. Regular meditation practice helps reduce depressive symptoms by improving emotional regulation and promoting a non-judgmental attitude towards one's thoughts and feelings. These effects are particularly important for those seeking alternatives to medication for managing depression.

Anxiety is another mental disorder that can be significantly alleviated through meditation. Researchers at Johns Hopkins University conducted a systematic review and meta-analysis of clinical studies, concluding that mindfulness meditation has a positive effect on anxiety. Participants in the studies who practiced meditation regularly reported a reduction in anxiety symptoms and a greater ability to manage stressful situations. This is particularly relevant in an era where anxiety disorders are among the most common mental health issues globally.

Studies have also examined the impact of meditation on emotional regulation and resilience. Meditative practice enhances the ability to recognize and understand one's emotions, reducing emotional reactivity and increasing the capacity to respond more balanced and adaptively to life stresses. This improved emotional competence contributes to greater resilience, allowing individuals to face adversity with greater strength and flexibility. A study conducted by the University of California, Davis, found that meditators showed a reduction in the stress hormone cortisol, along with greater emotional stability.

Meditation can also improve cognitive function and memory. Studies have shown that mindfulness practice increases the density of gray matter in brain areas associated with memory and learning. This suggests that meditation not only helps maintain a calm mind but can also enhance cognitive abilities, improving concentration and the ability to process and remember information.

Another significant mental health benefit of meditation is improved sleep. Numerous studies have shown that meditation can reduce symptoms of insomnia and improve sleep quality. Mindfulness practice helps calm the mind, reducing anxious thoughts that often interfere with sleep. Quality sleep is crucial for mental health, as it directly affects mood, memory, and the ability to handle stress.

In summary, scientific research has demonstrated that meditation offers a wide range of mental health benefits, including the reduction of stress, anxiety, and depression, improvement in emotional regulation and resilience, enhancement of cognitive function and sleep quality. These positive effects make meditation a powerful and accessible practice for promoting psychological well-being and improving quality of life.

Practical Meditation Exercises to Enhance the Quantum Mind

Enhancing the quantum mind through meditation involves practical exercises that refine awareness and intention. These exercises not only improve mental and physical well-being but also our ability to perceive and interact with the world on a deeper level. Here are some meditation techniques that can be particularly effective in developing a quantum mind.

A fundamental exercise is mindful breathing meditation. This exercise involves focusing all attention on the breath, observing the inhalation and exhalation without trying to control them. Sitting in a comfortable position, close your eyes and begin to follow the natural rhythm of your breath. Whenever the mind wanders, gently bring your attention back to the breath. This simple yet powerful exercise helps calm the mind, reduce stress, and develop a deeper awareness of the present moment. Practiced regularly, it can enhance concentration and mental clarity, essential elements for a quantum mind.

Another effective technique is creative visualization meditation. This exercise involves vividly imagining positive and desired scenarios. For example, you can visualize a personal or professional goal as if it has already been achieved, engaging all senses to make the experience as realistic as possible. Imagine the details, such as sounds, colors, and emotions associated with achieving that goal. This practice helps to program the brain to recognize and seize opportunities that lead to that result. It strengthens intention and determination, enhancing the ability to manifest your desires.

Metta meditation, or loving-kindness meditation, is an exercise that cultivates feelings of love, compassion, and connection with others. Sitting comfortably, close your eyes and silently repeat phrases such as "May I be happy," "May I be healthy," "May I live with ease." After cultivating these feelings for yourself, extend loving-kindness to others, starting with loved ones and then including acquaintances, strangers, and finally all of humanity. This exercise not only improves emotional well-being but also expands the ability to perceive the connection between all living beings, a key principle of the quantum mind.

Body scan meditation is another useful practice for enhancing the quantum mind. This exercise involves bringing mindful attention to different parts of the body, noticing sensations without judgment. Lying down or sitting, close your eyes and start focusing attention on the feet, then gradually move up the body, passing through the legs, abdomen, chest, arms, neck, and head. This exercise helps develop greater body awareness, release tensions, and promote deep relaxation. Body scan meditation also grounds you in the present moment, improving the ability to perceive and react to subtle mind-body connections.

Gratitude meditation is a powerful exercise to cultivate a quantum mind. Each day, spend a few minutes reflecting on what you are grateful for, writing it in a journal or simply contemplating it silently. Gratitude helps focus attention on the positive aspects of life, promoting an attitude of abundance and openness. This practice not only improves mood and emotional well-being but also strengthens the perception of being part of a universe rich in infinite possibilities.

These meditation exercises—mindful breathing, creative visualization, Metta meditation, body scan, and gratitude meditation—offer practical tools to enhance the quantum mind. Practiced regularly, they help develop deep awareness, strengthen intention, and cultivate a harmonious connection between mind and body, facilitating the ability to perceive and interact with the world more consciously and intentionally.

Chapter 10

Invisible Connections in Relationships

The Importance of Mental and Emotional Connections in Human Relationships

Mental and emotional connections play a crucial role in human relationships, profoundly influencing the quality and depth of our interactions. These connections not only enable us to understand and feel understood by others but also help us develop meaningful bonds that enrich our lives and enhance our well-being.

At the heart of mental and emotional connections is empathy, the ability to put oneself in another's shoes and perceive their feelings and thoughts. Empathy creates a bridge between people, allowing them to share emotional experiences and feel closer to one another. When we can perceive and understand others' emotions, we can respond more appropriately and compassionately, strengthening the emotional bond. This is especially important in intimate relationships, where empathy helps build a foundation of trust and mutual understanding.

Authentic communication is another fundamental element for establishing strong mental and emotional connections. The ability to express thoughts and feelings clearly and honestly facilitates creating an environment where people feel safe and respected. Open and sincere communication allows for addressing and resolving conflicts constructively, avoiding misunderstandings and resentments. This type of communication involves not only words but also body language, tone of voice, and active listening, all of which contribute to a deeper and more authentic understanding of each other.

Mental and emotional connections are also crucial for mutual support. In times of difficulty or stress, knowing that someone understands and shares our feelings can make a significant difference. This kind of emotional support not only alleviates suffering but also strengthens the bond between people. Relationships with strong emotional support are often more resilient and rewarding because they are based on mutual understanding and assistance.

Another important aspect of mental and emotional connections is their ability to promote personal growth. Deep and meaningful relationships offer opportunities to learn more about ourselves through interaction with others. Shared experiences and feedback from loved ones help us reflect on our behaviors, values, and goals. This process of reflection and learning is essential for personal development and improving our relationships.

Mental and emotional connections are not limited to romantic or familial relationships but also extend to friendships and professional relationships. In every context, the ability to connect deeply with others enhances collaboration, creativity, and overall satisfaction. In the workplace, for example, emotional connections among colleagues can create a more positive and productive environment, increasing the sense of belonging and motivation.

The practice of mindfulness can be an effective tool for cultivating these connections. Mindfulness teaches us to be present and aware in our interactions, allowing us to listen and respond with greater attention and compassion. This mindful presence enhances the quality of our relationships, making them more authentic and meaningful.

Finally, mental and emotional connections contribute to our psychological and physical well-being. Numerous studies have shown that people with strong, positive relationships tend to be happier, less stressed, and live longer. The feeling of being understood and supported creates a sense of security and belonging essential for our mental and physical health.

In conclusion, mental and emotional connections are fundamental to the quality of our relationships and our overall well-being. These connections enable us to understand and feel understood, support and be supported, and grow together with others. Cultivating these connections requires empathy, authentic communication, and mindful presence, but the benefits are immeasurable, profoundly enriching our lives and those of others.

Theories and Research on Energetic and Quantum Connections Between People

Theories and research on energetic and quantum connections between people delve into a fascinating and complex field, aiming to understand how individuals may be interconnected at a deeper, less visible level. These connections transcend physical and verbal interactions, suggesting that invisible bonds influence our experiences and relationships.

One of the most discussed theories is quantum entanglement. This phenomenon, observed in quantum physics, describes how two particles can remain interconnected regardless of the distance between them. Changes in the state of one particle are instantaneously reflected in the other, suggesting a connection that transcends space. Some researchers and theorists propose that a similar principle could apply to human relationships, where people's minds and energies remain interconnected in subtle but significant ways.

Dean Radin, a leading researcher at the Institute of Noetic Sciences, has conducted experiments to explore these non-local connections between people. In one study, participants were placed in separate rooms, and their physiological responses, such as skin conductance, were monitored while one participant was exposed to emotional stimuli. The results showed that the physiological responses were synchronized, suggesting an invisible connection that allows emotions to be shared at a distance.

Another area of research focuses on so-called "energetic connections" between people. This concept is rooted in spiritual and holistic traditions that claim the existence of human energy fields, often referred to as the "aura" or "bioenergetic field." According to these traditions, these energy fields can interact and influence each other. Beverly Rubik, a biophysicist, has studied the human bioenergetic field and found evidence suggesting that these fields can vary in response to emotions and intentions, indicating that energetic connections between people can influence well-being and relationships.

Research on collective consciousness is another intriguing dimension of quantum connections between people. The Global Consciousness Project, initiated by Roger Nelson at Princeton University, monitors a global network of random number generators to detect fluctuations during events of significant worldwide emotional impact, such as terrorist attacks or mass celebrations. The results showed that during these events, the data deviated from expected randomness, suggesting that human collective consciousness can influence physical systems at a distance.

Experiences of synchronicity, introduced by Carl Jung, offer further reflection. Synchronicity refers to meaningful coincidences that cannot be explained by conventional causes. These events often seem to connect minds and situations in surprising and profound ways, suggesting that quantum or energetic connections are at play beyond our current understanding.

Finally, energetic healing practices such as Reiki and Qi Gong are based on the idea that vital energy can be channeled and transmitted between people to promote healing. Preliminary studies have suggested that such practices can have positive effects on physical and mental well-being, providing further indication that real energetic connections exist between individuals.

In summary, theories and research on energetic and quantum connections between people open new frontiers in our understanding of human relationships.

These connections, although invisible, seem to have a tangible impact on our experiences and well-being. Exploring and better understanding these interactions could revolutionize our approach to relationships, healing, and self-awareness, leading us to recognize the profound interconnectedness that exists among all human beings.

Examples of Empathy and Synchronicity in Relationships

Empathy and synchronicity are phenomena that profoundly enrich human relationships, revealing the complexity and beauty of the invisible connections that bind us to one another. Exploring concrete examples of empathy and synchronicity in relationships can help us better understand how these subtle forces influence our daily interactions.

Empathy is the ability to understand and share the feelings of others. This phenomenon often manifests in extraordinary ways in close relationships. For instance, imagine two friends who have known each other for years. One of them, without knowing exactly why, begins to feel worried and uneasy. Shortly afterward, they receive a call from the friend who is going through a difficult time. This type of empathetic experience, where one person intuitively perceives the emotional state of the other, is surprisingly common among individuals who share deep bonds.

Another example of empathy can be found in parent-child relationships. Many mothers report "feeling" when their children are in danger or need them, even when there are no obvious external signals. This deep empathetic bond can be seen as a form of quantum or energetic connection, where one person's emotions and needs directly influence the other's perception. Such experiences strengthen the bond between parents and children, creating a sense of mutual security and protection.

Synchronicity, a concept introduced by psychologist Carl Jung, refers to meaningful coincidences that seem to have a profound but non-causal connection. A classic example of synchronicity in relationships can be seen in stories of fortuitous meetings. Consider the story of two people who, after years of distance and no contact, randomly meet in a foreign city, discovering that they have gone through parallel life experiences and need each other at that precise moment. This coincidence seems orchestrated by a larger force, suggesting that their lives are intertwined in mysterious and significant ways.

Experiences of synchronicity can also manifest through small daily events that, taken individually, seem insignificant but together create a picture of meaningful connections. For example, a person might think intensely about a friend they haven't seen in a long time, only to receive a message or call from that friend shortly afterward. These coincidences create a sense of wonder and connection, making people feel part of a broader network of meaningful relationships.

Empathetic and synchronous experiences can also profoundly influence romantic relationships. Imagine a couple who, despite physical distance, continue to share intense and synchronous emotional experiences. One partner might wake up from a disturbing dream only to find that the other had a sleepless night due to similar worries. These moments of synchronicity and empathetic connection strengthen the bond between partners, creating a sense of unity and understanding that goes beyond verbal communication.

Another example of empathy and synchronicity can be found in deep friendships. Two friends who have gone through tough times together often develop an intuitive understanding of each other. They might finish each other's sentences, know exactly what to say in times of crisis, or share feelings without needing words. This empathetic and synchronous connection not only enriches the relationship but also offers vital emotional support, strengthening the bond of friendship.

In summary, empathy and synchronicity are fundamental elements that enrich human relationships, revealing the deep and often invisible connections that unite us. These phenomena not only enhance mutual understanding and emotional support but also create a sense of wonder and belonging, strengthening bonds and making relationships more meaningful and fulfilling. Exploring and recognizing these connections can transform how we perceive and experience our daily interactions, leading to greater awareness and appreciation of the wonders of human relationships.

Techniques for Enhancing Interpersonal Connection and Communication

Improving interpersonal connection and communication is fundamental for building strong and meaningful relationships. Approaches based on quantum mind principles offer innovative techniques that integrate concepts from quantum physics with mental awareness, enabling more effective and profound communication.

A central aspect is the practice of mindful presence. Being fully present during interactions means dedicating complete attention to the other person, eliminating internal and external distractions. This not only improves the quality of communication but also creates an energetic field of reciprocity. According to quantum physics principles, the observer influences the observed system. Being fully present can positively alter the dynamics of the conversation, facilitating a more authentic and harmonious connection.

Another effective technique is active listening, which involves the quantum mind in the act of listening. Active listening requires understanding not just the words but also the underlying emotions and intentions. This type of listening goes beyond simple auditory perception; it requires full attention and an empathetic response. Quantum physics teaches us that subatomic particles communicate and interact instantly over a distance. Similarly, active listening can create an immediate and deep connection between people, facilitating understanding and conflict resolution.

Synchronizing energies is another powerful tool. Techniques such as meditation and synchronized breathing can help align energies between people. For example, before an important conversation, taking a few minutes to breathe together in silence can harmonize energetic frequencies. This process, similar to quantum entanglement, where particles remain connected regardless of distance, can improve coherence and mutual understanding.

Visualization is a useful technique for enhancing interpersonal connection. Imagining positive scenarios of communication and interaction can prepare the mind to respond more effectively and compassionately. Creative visualization leverages the principle of quantum superposition, where every possible state exists until it is observed. By visualizing positive interactions, you can influence the likelihood of realizing them, creating a more harmonious reality in relationships.

Non-verbal communication plays a crucial role in interpersonal connection. Being aware of body language, facial expressions, and tone of voice can significantly improve the quality of interactions. According to quantum theory, information can be transmitted and received through unconventional channels. Paying attention to non-verbal communication allows you to perceive these subtle energetic connections, facilitating a more complete and intuitive understanding of the other person.

Another effective tool is the practice of gratitude and acknowledgment. Expressing sincere appreciation for the qualities and actions of the other person strengthens the emotional bond and creates a positive atmosphere. Quantum physics teaches us that positive energies attract further positive energies, creating a virtuous cycle. Cultivating an attitude of gratitude not only improves the relationship but also enhances the overall well-being of the people involved.

Finally, awareness of intention is fundamental for improving interpersonal connection. Being clear about your intentions and communicating them transparently can prevent misunderstandings and build trust. Quantum physics suggests that intentions influence reality at a subatomic level. Similarly, in human relationships, clear and positive intentions can shape interactions in a constructive and meaningful way.

In summary, techniques based on the quantum mind offer powerful tools for enhancing interpersonal connection and communication. By integrating mindful presence, active listening, energy synchronization, visualization, non-verbal communication, gratitude, and intentional awareness, you can create deeper and more meaningful relationships. These practices enrich the quality of your life and your daily interactions, fostering a sense of connection and understanding that transcends traditional communication methods.

The Role of Emotions and Intentions in Invisible Connections

Emotions and intentions play a fundamental role in the invisible connections between people, profoundly influencing the quality and depth of our interactions. These connections, viewed through the lens of the quantum mind, reveal how our emotional experiences and intentions can subtly but powerfully shape reality.

Emotions are powerful energies that can affect not only our mood but also the people around us. Quantum physics suggests that everything in the universe is interconnected at a subatomic level, and human emotions are no exception. When we experience intense emotions such as love, joy, or anger, we emit an energetic "vibration" that can be perceived by others. These vibrations can create energetic fields that influence the behavior and perceptions of those we interact with. For instance, in a romantic relationship, deep love between partners can create an energetic field of connection that strengthens the bond and promotes mutual understanding.

Emotions can also act as catalysts for synchronicity—those moments of meaningful coincidence that seem orchestrated by an invisible force. When we are emotionally attuned to someone, we are more likely to experience synchronicities in our interactions. This might manifest as similar thoughts, shared intuitions, or fortuitous encounters that seem too perfect to be mere coincidences. Quantum physics, with its principles of non-locality and entanglement, offers a possible explanation for these experiences, suggesting that emotions can create instantaneous connections that transcend time and space.

Intentions are equally powerful in shaping invisible connections. Intentions represent the direction of our mental and emotional energy toward a specific goal. When we formulate a clear and focused intention, we send an energetic signal into the universe that can influence events and people around us. This principle underlies many spiritual and self-help practices, such as creative visualization and the law of attraction. Quantum physics supports the idea that the observer can influence the observed system, suggesting that our intentions can indeed shape reality.

In a relationship, intentions play a crucial role in determining the quality of the connection. When both parties in a relationship have the intention to build trust, understanding, and mutual support, these intentions create a positive energetic field that facilitates growth and harmony. Intentions can also help resolve conflicts, as the intention to understand and address issues constructively creates a space of openness and cooperation.

A tangible example of the power of emotions and intentions in invisible connections can be seen in energy healing practices, such as Reiki. Reiki practitioners intentionally channel healing energy toward the recipient, aiming to balance their energy field and promote healing. The positive effects reported by recipients suggest that the practitioner's focused intentions, combined with positive emotional energy, can have a real and tangible impact on physical and mental well-being.

Emotions and intentions also influence our perception of reality. When we cultivate positive emotions such as gratitude and love and formulate positive intentions, our perception of the world tends to become brighter and more optimistic. This perceptual shift not only enhances our personal well-being but also creates a ripple effect, positively influencing the people around us. Quantum physics suggests that the observer and the observed are interconnected, and this principle perfectly applies to how our emotions and intentions shape our daily experiences.

To build deeper and more meaningful connections, it's essential to recognize and cultivate the power of emotions and intentions. Here are some techniques to enhance these connections:

Mindful Presence: Being fully present in interactions allows for genuine connections. This presence can positively alter the dynamic of the conversation, fostering authentic and harmonious connections.

Active Listening: Understanding the emotions and intentions behind words fosters deep connections. This type of listening creates an immediate and profound bond, facilitating understanding and conflict resolution.

Energy Synchronization: Techniques like synchronized breathing before conversations can harmonize energetic frequencies, improving coherence and mutual understanding.

Visualization: Imagining positive interaction scenarios prepares the mind for compassionate responses, potentially manifesting harmonious realities in relationships.

Non-Verbal Communication: Awareness of body language, facial expressions, and tone enhances interaction quality, facilitating deeper understanding and connection.

Gratitude and Acknowledgment: Expressing sincere appreciation strengthens emotional bonds, creating a positive atmosphere that enhances overall relationship quality.

Intentional Awareness: Clear, positive intentions shape interactions constructively, fostering trust and deeper connections.

In conclusion, emotions and intentions are powerful forces that profoundly influence the invisible connections between people. Through the lens of the quantum mind, we can see how these energies create fields of connection that transcend time and space, shaping reality in deep and meaningful ways. Recognizing and cultivating these forces allows us to build deeper and more meaningful relationships, enhancing the quality of our lives and our daily interactions.

Chapter 11

Practical Applications of the Quantum Mind

Techniques of Visualization and Manifestation Based on Quantum Principles

The techniques of visualization and manifestation based on quantum principles represent a powerful approach to transforming desires and goals into reality. These practices draw on the foundations of quantum physics, particularly the notion that the observer influences the observed system and that reality consists of a multitude of possibilities until observed.

Creative visualization is one of the most effective techniques in this field. It involves creating vivid and detailed mental images of the goals we wish to achieve, engaging all the senses to make the experience as real as possible. For example, if you desire to obtain a new job, you can imagine yourself sitting at your ideal desk, feeling the excitement of the office environment, and hearing the sounds of your new workplace. This practice not only helps clarify goals but also activates the brain to recognize and attract opportunities that lead to the realization of these goals according to quantum principles.

An essential aspect of visualization is the vibration frequency. Every thought and emotion emits a frequency that can influence the surrounding energy field. Cultivating positive thoughts and emotions during visualization elevates our vibration frequency, aligning it with what we wish to manifest. This principle is supported by quantum physics, which suggests that everything in the universe is energy and that similar energies attract each other. Visualizing with positive emotions such as gratitude, joy, and love amplifies the power of manifestation.

Another effective technique is focused intention. This method is based on clearly and specifically formulating intentions, followed by visualizing the desired outcome as if it has already been achieved. Intentions act as energetic signals sent into the universe, influencing the quantum field to create favorable circumstances for achieving our goals. Quantum physics suggests that observation can collapse the wave function into a concrete reality. Similarly, focused intention can help materialize desires by transforming potentials into reality.

Positive affirmations are another technique that can be used alongside visualization. Repeating positive and empowering phrases helps reprogram the subconscious mind, aligning our thoughts with our goals. Affirmations work as mental anchors that strengthen our belief in the possibility of achieving our desires. For instance, repeating "I am worthy of success and attract it easily" can boost self-confidence and create a positive mental attitude that facilitates manifestation.

Quantum meditation is a technique that combines elements of visualization, intention, and mindfulness. During meditation, one enters a state of deep relaxation and focuses on desired goals, visualizing them clearly and involving all positive emotions associated with their achievement. This meditative state allows access to deeper levels of the mind, where the barriers between the conscious and subconscious are reduced. Quantum meditation facilitates the alignment of internal energy frequencies with those of the universe, enhancing the chances of manifestation.

Finally, the manifestation journal is a practical method that helps maintain focus on goals. Writing down desires daily and visualizing them as already realized reinforces intention and mental clarity. This writing process not only solidifies goals in the mind but also acts as a ritual that keeps the vibration frequency high, helping to maintain a positive and focused attitude.

In conclusion, the techniques of visualization and manifestation based on quantum principles offer powerful tools for transforming desires into reality. By integrating creative visualization, focused intention, positive affirmations, quantum meditation, and the manifestation journal, one can harness the power of the quantum mind to influence reality in a significant way. These practices not only improve mental and emotional well-being but also open new possibilities for achieving personal dreams and goals.

Strategies for Using the Quantum Mind to Achieve Goals

Using the quantum mind to achieve goals involves integrating principles of quantum physics with personal development techniques. This method is based on the idea that reality is influenced by our intentions and awareness, and we can leverage this interaction to realize our desires.

A key strategy is the clear and precise definition of goals. Quantum physics teaches us that focused observation can influence the behavior of subatomic particles, suggesting that a clear vision of our goals can catalyze the manifestation process. Taking the time to define exactly what you want to achieve, writing it down in detail, helps create a mental map that guides daily actions and decisions towards achieving those goals.

Creative visualization is another powerful strategy. Vividly imagining the achievement of your goals, involving all the senses, helps program the mind to recognize and seize opportunities that arise. This process, based on quantum superposition, allows you to mentally explore different possibilities until one of them materializes in reality. Visualizing success with positive emotions reinforces determination and motivates you to persevere despite difficulties.

Focused intention is fundamental in utilizing the quantum mind. Clear and well-defined intentions act as signals that influence the quantum field. Formulating and repeating positive intentions daily helps maintain focus on goals, creating alignment between thoughts, emotions, and actions. This principle is similar to the observer effect in quantum physics, where the act of observing changes the outcome of the observation. Similarly, maintaining focused intention can direct mental energy towards achieving goals.

Meditation is another practice that facilitates the use of the quantum mind. Regular meditation helps calm the mind, reduce stress, and increase awareness. During meditation, you can focus on your goals, visualizing them as already achieved. This state of deep awareness allows access to subtler levels of the mind, where barriers between the conscious and subconscious are reduced. Meditation facilitates the integration of intentions at the subconscious level, strengthening the ability to manifest desires.

The importance of positive affirmations cannot be underestimated. Affirmations are powerful phrases that influence the subconscious mind and help maintain a positive mental attitude. Repeating affirmations like "I am capable of achieving my goals" or "I attract success and abundance into my life" helps reprogram the mind, eliminating limiting beliefs and reinforcing self-confidence. This process is similar to observation in quantum physics, where the observer's expectations can influence the experiment's outcome.

Inspired action is another essential strategy. The quantum mind involves not just visualization and intention, but also concrete action. Listening to intuition and acting when perceiving signals or opportunities is crucial for the manifestation process. Intuitions often derive from a deep level of awareness and can guide you toward actions that perfectly align with desired goals. Acting with confidence and decisiveness creates an energy flow that promotes goal achievement.

Finally, gratitude is a powerful practice that enhances the use of the quantum mind. Being grateful for what you have and the progress made elevates your vibrational frequency and attracts further positive experiences. Gratitude helps maintain an attitude of abundance and openness, fostering a virtuous cycle of success and fulfillment.

In summary, the strategies for using the quantum mind to achieve goals combine clear goal setting, creative visualization, focused intention, meditation, positive affirmations, inspired action, and gratitude. These practices, rooted in quantum physics principles, offer an integrated approach to transforming desires into reality, significantly improving life quality and the ability to achieve personal goals.

Personal and Professional Success Stories Thanks to the Quantum Mind

The concept of the quantum mind has led many individuals to experience extraordinary successes in both personal and professional spheres. These examples demonstrate how applying the principles of quantum physics can profoundly transform lives.

Take the case of Sarah, a young entrepreneur in the tech industry. Initially, Sarah struggled to get her startup off the ground. Despite having an innovative idea, she lacked visibility and resources. She decided to adopt techniques of visualization and focused intention. Every morning, she dedicated time to imagining her company's success: she saw herself presenting the product to an enthusiastic audience, felt the excitement of the crowd, and perceived the satisfaction of closing important deals. Additionally, she formulated clear and positive intentions, such as "I attract clients and investors who believe in my project."

Over time, she noticed significant changes. Her presentations improved, becoming more engaging and persuasive. Through networking events, she met a key investor who became passionate about her project and decided to fund her startup. This fortuitous meeting seemed orchestrated by an invisible force, confirming to Sarah the effectiveness of her quantum practices. Today, her company is an international success, and she attributes much of her triumph to the consistent practice of visualization and intention.

Another success story related to the quantum mind is that of Marco, a marketing professional. Marco felt stuck in his career, unable to advance despite his skills. He decided to explore quantum meditation and positive affirmations. Every day, he meditated on images of himself achieving specific professional goals, such as obtaining promotions and managing important projects. He repeated affirmations like "I am an effective and recognized leader in my field."

Within a few months, he began to notice opportunities that previously seemed out of reach. A high-visibility project was assigned to Marco, allowing him to demonstrate his value and secure a promotion. His new position enabled him to further develop his skills and lead the team to success. Marco acknowledges that his practice of meditation and affirmations played a crucial role in his career transformation, helping him maintain a positive and proactive attitude, attracting opportunities aligned with his intentions.

In the personal realm, the quantum approach can lead to significant transformations. Laura, a young mother, felt overwhelmed by responsibilities and lacked time for herself. She decided to dedicate a few minutes each day to meditation and gratitude practice. She visualized a balanced life, where she successfully managed family demands while finding time for her passions. She expressed gratitude for small things, such as joyful moments with her children and the support of her partner.

These practices led to a shift in perspective. Laura began to notice more positive moments in her day and felt less stressed. Over time, she managed to better organize her activities, finding space to practice yoga and read, activities that gave her energy and satisfaction. This renewed balance improved not only her personal well-being but also the quality of her family relationships.

These examples demonstrate how adopting quantum techniques can transform both career and personal life.

Through visualization, focused intention, meditation, and gratitude, individuals like Sarah, Marco, and Laura have harnessed the power of the quantum mind to attract success and fulfillment, confirming the effectiveness of these practices in shaping reality and achieving their goals.

How to Integrate the Practice of the Quantum Mind into Daily Life

Integrating the practice of the quantum mind into daily life can profoundly transform how we approach our experiences and goals. This approach is based on the principles of quantum physics, which suggest that our reality is influenced by our intentions and observations. Here are some practical strategies for incorporating these concepts into the daily routine, enhancing well-being and personal success.

One of the first steps is to start the day with a session of creative visualization. Upon waking, spend a few minutes vividly imagining your goals as already achieved. For instance, if you desire to improve your career, visualize yourself in your ideal work environment, performing tasks you love, and receiving recognition for your contributions. This practice not only helps clarify goals but also aligns the mind with the positive frequencies necessary to attract opportunities.

Daily meditation is another essential tool. Meditation helps calm the mind, reduce stress, and increase awareness. Finding a quiet moment in the day, even for just 10-15 minutes, can make a significant difference. During meditation, focus on your breath and observe your thoughts without judgment. Integrating specific intentions into the meditative moment, such as "Today I attract abundance and positivity," can amplify the power of manifestation, influencing the quantum field around you.

Using positive affirmations is a powerful technique to reprogram the subconscious mind. Repeating affirmations throughout the day helps maintain a positive and focused mental attitude. Phrases like "I am capable of overcoming any obstacle" or "I deserve success and happiness" reinforce self-confidence and align energies with desired goals. This practice, similar to the quantum concept of the observer influencing the observed, helps create a reality where your desires can materialize.

Gratitude is another key element. Practicing daily gratitude, perhaps by keeping a journal where you note things you are thankful for, elevates your vibrational frequency and attracts further positive experiences. Gratitude helps maintain an attitude of abundance and openness, facilitating the manifestation of desires. Before going to bed, reflect on three positive things that happened during the day and feel grateful for each. This exercise not only improves mood but also strengthens the connection with the positive energy of the universe.

Inspired action is crucial for integrating the quantum mind into daily life. Besides visualization and intentions, concrete action is essential. Listen to intuition and act when you perceive signals or opportunities. If you feel an urge to contact someone or attend an event, follow that feeling. These moments of intuition often stem from a deeper awareness and can lead to unexpected and valuable opportunities.

Finally, cultivating positive relationships and surrounding yourself with people who support and share a similar vision of life can amplify the effect of quantum practices. The energies of those around us significantly influence our energy field. Maintaining relationships that elevate and inspire helps keep your vibrations high, facilitating the manifestation of desires.

Integrating the practice of the quantum mind into daily life requires consistency and awareness, but the benefits are profound and lasting. Through visualization, meditation, positive affirmations, gratitude, inspired action, and positive relationships, you can harness the principles of quantum physics to enhance your reality, attract success and fulfillment, and live a more harmonious and satisfying life.

Potential Challenges and How to Overcome Them in Practical Application

Applying the principles of the quantum mind in daily life can lead to extraordinary personal and professional transformations. However, as with any practice, challenges may arise. Recognizing and addressing these difficulties is essential to maximize the benefits of the quantum mind and ensure continuous growth.

One of the main challenges is maintaining consistency. While integrating practices such as visualization, meditation, and affirmations into a daily routine, many people initially find enthusiasm and motivation. However, over time, maintaining discipline can become difficult. The quantum mind, which requires consistent commitment to positively influence reality, can be hindered by periods of distraction or stress. To overcome this challenge, it is helpful to establish a well-defined routine and create an environment that encourages regular practice. For example, dedicating a corner of the house to meditation and visualization can help create a daily ritual.

Another common challenge is dealing with doubts and limiting beliefs. Many people struggle with self-sabotage, questioning the validity of quantum techniques and their ability to manifest their desires. Quantum physics suggests that our beliefs influence reality, so doubts can hinder the manifestation process. To address this challenge, it is crucial to work on changing limiting beliefs. Positive affirmations and the constant repetition of empowering phrases can help reprogram the subconscious mind, replacing negative thoughts with beliefs of possibility and success.

Managing expectations is another obstacle to consider. Some may expect immediate results from their quantum practices, and when these do not manifest quickly, they may feel discouraged. It is important to understand that the manifestation process takes time and that profound changes often occur gradually. Patience and perseverance are essential. Keeping a manifestation journal, noting progress and synchronicities that occur along the way, can help maintain motivation and celebrate successes, even small ones.

Another challenge is integrating quantum practices into a busy modern life. Daily responsibilities, work commitments, and family obligations can leave little room for the practice of the quantum mind. To overcome this obstacle, it is helpful to incorporate these practices into existing moments of the day. For example, practicing gratitude during the commute, visualizing goals before sleeping, or meditating for a few minutes during a break. This approach makes quantum practices more accessible and less burdensome, promoting greater integration into daily life.

Resistance to change is another significant challenge. The human mind tends to prefer familiarity and may resist changes, even positive ones. Quantum physics teaches us that change is a constant and that adaptability is crucial for growth. Addressing this resistance requires a gradual approach. Starting with small changes and gradually increasing the intensity and duration of quantum practices can help overcome resistance. Additionally, seeking support from communities or groups with similar interests can provide encouragement and motivation, making the change process more sustainable.

Finally, the challenge of the lack of immediate tangible evidence can undermine confidence in quantum practices. Quantum physics often operates on subtle and invisible levels, and results may not be immediately evident. Maintaining trust in the process, despite the absence of immediate proof, is fundamental. Practices such as daily reflection and mindfulness can help notice subtle changes and keep motivation alive.

In conclusion, addressing and overcoming challenges in the application of the quantum mind requires commitment, patience, and adaptability. Establishing a routine, working on limiting beliefs, managing expectations, integrating practices into daily life, addressing resistance to change, and maintaining trust in the process are all essential elements for effectively using quantum principles and transforming one's reality.

Chapter 12

The Future of the Quantum Mind

Future Prospects for Research on Connections Between the Mind and Quantum Physics

The future prospects for research on the connections between the mind and quantum physics promise to revolutionize our understanding of consciousness, reality, and human interactions. This emerging field, situated at the intersection of neuroscience, psychology, and physics, explores how quantum principles might explain complex mental phenomena and open new pathways for enhancing human well-being.

One of the most promising areas of research concerns quantum entanglement and its potential role in mental and emotional connections. Entanglement describes a situation where two particles, once interconnected, remain linked regardless of the distance separating them. Some scientists hypothesize that a similar phenomenon could exist between human minds, allowing for instantaneous, non-local communication. Future studies could focus on exploring this hypothesis using advanced brain imaging techniques and brainwave measurement tools to search for evidence of quantum connections between individuals.

Another fascinating perspective involves the possibility that fundamental brain processes operate at the quantum level. Researchers like physicist Roger Penrose and physician Stuart Hameroff have proposed that consciousness might result from quantum processes within the microtubules of brain cells. This theory, known as "Orchestrated Objective Reduction" (Orch-OR), suggests that the human mind could be directly linked to quantum dynamics. Future research in this direction could provide new insights into the workings of consciousness and pave the way for advanced technologies to enhance cognitive function and treat neurological diseases.

The implications of quantum physics for psychology and therapy are equally promising. Integrating quantum principles into therapeutic practices could lead to new methods for addressing mental disorders and improving emotional well-being. For example, visualization and meditation techniques based on the quantum mind could be used to treat anxiety, depression, and post-traumatic stress disorder. Future research could explore the effectiveness of these approaches, conducting clinical trials to assess their impact and develop therapeutic protocols based on quantum physics.

The connection between the mind and quantum physics could also revolutionize the field of artificial intelligence (AI). Advances in quantum computing offer the potential to create AI systems that operate according to principles similar to those of the human brain. These systems could solve complex problems with unprecedented speed and accuracy, opening new frontiers in fields such as medicine, scientific research, and technology. Collaboration between neuroscientists, physicists, and computer engineers could lead to the creation of machines that not only emulate the human mind but surpass it in analytical and creative capabilities.

Finally, research on the connections between the mind and quantum physics could have profound implications for our understanding of reality and our place in the universe. Discoveries in this field could redefine fundamental concepts such as free will, the nature of time and space, and the meaning of life itself. Exploring these themes could usher in a new era of awareness and understanding, where science and spirituality converge to offer a more complete and integrated vision of reality.

In conclusion, the future prospects for research on the connections between the mind and quantum physics are extremely promising. This interdisciplinary field could revolutionize our understanding of consciousness, improve therapeutic practices, advance artificial intelligence, and transform our vision of reality. With the progress of technology and increased collaboration among scientists from various disciplines, we are on the threshold of discoveries that could profoundly change our understanding of the world and the human mind.

Ethical and Social Implications of Discoveries in This Field

The discoveries about the connections between the mind and quantum physics bring a series of ethical and social implications that deserve thorough consideration. These implications can affect various aspects of our lives, from individual privacy and autonomy to social inequalities and access to technology.

One major ethical issue concerns mental privacy. If research proves that human minds can be interconnected at a quantum level, there might be risks of unauthorized interference or manipulation of thoughts and emotions. For instance, advanced technologies could theoretically be developed to read or influence brain waves, threatening our mental autonomy. It is essential for legislation and regulations to evolve to protect mental privacy, ensuring these technologies are used ethically and respectfully of individual rights.

The social implications of such discoveries could also exacerbate existing inequalities. Access to technologies based on quantum mind principles might be limited to those with sufficient financial resources, creating an even wider gap between the rich and the poor. Technologies that enhance cognitive abilities or improve stress and emotion management could become tools of power, used to maintain or increase social control. It is crucial that these innovations are made accessible to all, regardless of socioeconomic status, to prevent new forms of inequality and injustice from emerging.

Discoveries in the field of the quantum mind could also influence our understanding of identity and free will. If the mind is influenced by quantum processes, it might suggest that our choices and decisions are not entirely autonomous but rather the result of complex interactions at the subatomic level. This raises fundamental ethical questions about personal responsibility and the nature of free will. As a society, we should reflect on how these new insights might affect our conception of morality and justice and how they can be integrated into our legal and social structures.

The possibility of cognitive enhancements through quantum techniques raises further ethical dilemmas. The use of such technologies could be seen as a way to enhance human potential but might also lead to social pressures to conform to new standards of performance and productivity. The freedom to choose not to use such enhancements should be respected, and ethical guidelines should be developed to ensure that the use of these technologies is voluntary and non-coercive.

Another implication concerns mental health and well-being. Techniques based on the quantum mind could revolutionize the treatment of mental disorders, but they could also be misused or applied unethically. It is crucial that therapeutic applications are rigorously tested and regulated to ensure they are safe and effective. Additionally, we should consider the psychological impact of such technologies on individuals, ensuring they are used to promote well-being rather than to manipulate or control.

Finally, discoveries about the quantum mind might influence our conception of spirituality and human connection. If minds are interconnected at a quantum level, this could support ancient spiritual beliefs about the interconnectedness of all things. However, it is important that these discoveries are integrated in a respectful and inclusive manner, recognizing the diversity of spiritual and religious traditions and promoting an open and respectful dialogue between science and spirituality.

In summary, the ethical and social implications of discoveries about the connections between the mind and quantum physics are profound and complex. It is essential to address these issues carefully, ensuring that new knowledge and technologies are used ethically, equitably, and respectfully of the rights and dignity of all individuals. Only by doing so can we ensure that innovations in the field of the quantum mind contribute positively and sustainably to human progress.

New Technologies and Emerging Practices Inspired by the Quantum Mind

New technologies and emerging practices inspired by the quantum mind are opening unexplored frontiers in science, medicine, and personal development. These innovations, based on the principles of quantum physics, promise to transform our understanding of the mind and reality, offering advanced tools to enhance everyday life.

One of the most promising technologies is quantum computing. Unlike traditional computers, which process information in binary bits, quantum computers use qubits that can exist in multiple states simultaneously due to quantum superposition. This capability allows them to solve complex problems at unimaginable speeds for conventional computers. In the field of neuroscience, quantum computers could be used to model and simulate the functioning of the human brain with unprecedented precision, opening new possibilities for treating mental and neurological disorders.

Another significant innovation is brain-computer interfaces (BCIs), which leverage quantum mind principles to improve communication between the human brain and external devices. BCIs allow individuals to control computers and other devices simply by using their thoughts. This technology has revolutionary applications in the field of disability, offering new forms of independence and improving the quality of life for people with reduced mobility. Additionally, BCIs can be used to enhance cognitive abilities and improve learning, enabling more direct and intuitive interaction with technology.

Quantum medicine is an emerging field that applies the principles of quantum physics to the diagnosis and treatment of diseases. One of the most intriguing practices is quantum therapy, which uses energy frequencies to balance and harmonize the body at the subatomic level. This approach is based on the idea that every cell and organ in the human body emits a specific frequency and that disease can be seen as a distortion of these frequencies. Quantum therapy aims to restore energetic balance, promoting healing and well-being. Although still experimental, this practice is attracting the interest of researchers and doctors for its potential to revolutionize traditional medicine.

Quantum meditation is another emerging practice that combines traditional meditation techniques with the principles of quantum physics. This form of meditation focuses on aligning mental frequencies with those of the universe, facilitating a deep state of awareness and connection. Quantum meditation can enhance visualization skills, increase creativity, and promote a sense of unity with the whole. Practitioners report significant benefits, including greater mental calm, reduced stress, and improved overall well-being.

In the field of education, quantum technologies are beginning to influence how we learn and teach. Quantum simulators can be used to create immersive learning environments that allow students to explore complex concepts through interactive experiences. This approach not only facilitates a deeper understanding of scientific subjects but also stimulates students' interest and motivation. Integrating the quantum mind into education could lead to an era of personalized and adaptive learning, where each student can progress at their own pace and according to their needs.

Artificial neural networks, inspired by the quantum mind, are rapidly advancing in the field of artificial intelligence. These systems, which mimic the functioning of the human brain, can learn and adapt autonomously. Quantum artificial intelligence could surpass the capabilities of current systems, leading to extraordinary innovations in sectors such as healthcare, finance, and scientific research. Applications of these technologies range from early disease diagnosis to new drug discovery, from advanced financial management to solving complex scientific problems.

In conclusion, new technologies and emerging practices inspired by the quantum mind are opening extraordinary possibilities in various fields. These innovations, leveraging the principles of quantum physics, promise to revolutionize our understanding of the mind and reality, offering advanced tools to improve quality of life and promote well-being. With the continuous progress of research and technology, we are at the beginning of a new era of discovery and innovation that could radically transform our world.

Speculations on How These Discoveries Can Transform Society

Discoveries on the connections between the mind and quantum physics have the potential to transform society in profound and unexpected ways. These transformations could touch every aspect of our lives, from health and education to communication and work, creating a new and dynamic world.

In the field of health, the integration of quantum technologies and practices could revolutionize disease treatment. Imagine a future where doctors use devices based on quantum physics to diagnose diseases at early stages, treating them with energy therapies that restore balance at the subatomic level. This approach could drastically reduce the need for invasive drugs and surgery, improving the quality of life and increasing life expectancy. Quantum medicine could also promote a more holistic care model, where mental and emotional well-being is considered as essential as physical health.

In education, quantum technologies could transform learning into an immersive and personalized experience. Students could use quantum simulators to explore complex concepts through interactive virtual experiences, enhancing understanding and interest. This approach could make education more inclusive, adapting curricula to individual needs and paces. Schools of the future could become innovation centers where every student has the opportunity to explore their talents and interests, promoting a more creative and adaptable society.

Interpersonal communication could also undergo a radical transformation. If quantum connections between human minds were confirmed, we could develop new forms of technology-assisted telepathy, making communication more immediate and profound. This could improve mutual understanding and reduce conflicts, fostering more harmonious relationships. Language barriers could be overcome, allowing fluid communication between people of different cultures and promoting greater global cohesion.

In the world of work, the integration of quantum technologies could increase efficiency and creativity. Quantum computers could solve complex problems in seconds, accelerating innovation in fields such as scientific research, finance, and engineering design. Advanced automation, driven by quantum artificial intelligence, could free humans from repetitive tasks, allowing them to focus on more creative and strategic activities. This change could lead to a reduction in working hours and a greater emphasis on well-being and personal development.

Discoveries in the field of the quantum mind could also profoundly influence governance and politics. Understanding quantum connections between individuals could promote the development of more collaborative and consensus-based policies. Political decisions could be made considering the insights and perspectives of a broader range of individuals, using technologies that facilitate the collection and analysis of collective opinions. This approach could lead to more inclusive and representative governance, improving transparency and trust in the decision-making process.

Finally, the social transformation resulting from discoveries on the quantum mind could lead to greater awareness of our interconnectedness. If we recognize that we are all connected at a quantum level, we can develop a deeper sense of mutual responsibility and care for the planet. This could foster more sustainable behaviors and a collective commitment to address global challenges such as climate change, poverty, and inequality.

In summary, discoveries on the connections between the mind and quantum physics have the potential to profoundly transform society. From health to education, from communication to work, these innovations promise to create a more harmonious, inclusive, and aware world. The implications of these discoveries could lead to a future where science and spirituality unite to improve the quality of life and promote global well-being.

Conclusions and Final Reflections on the Journey Through the Quantum Mind

The journey through the quantum mind has led us to explore fascinating and complex territories where quantum physics intertwines with neuroscience, psychology, and philosophy to offer us a new understanding of reality and our place in it. This path has revealed not only the profound connections between mental processes and quantum principles but also the immense possibilities that open up for humanity.

We have seen how the principles of quantum physics, such as superposition, entanglement, and the observer effect, can explain complex mental phenomena and offer new perspectives on how the mind interacts with the world. These concepts invite us to consider that reality is not fixed and immutable but fluid and moldable through our intentions and perceptions. In this context, the mind becomes not just an instrument of observation but also of creation, capable of influencing and shaping the surrounding reality.

Integrating quantum practices into daily life, such as creative visualization, meditation, and positive affirmations, offers us practical tools to enhance our existence. These techniques teach us to harness the power of our intentions and channel our energies in ways that can lead to greater personal fulfillment and well-being. The awareness of our ability to influence reality also gives us a sense of personal responsibility and power, encouraging us to live more consciously and intentionally.

The ethical and social implications of discoveries about the quantum mind are equally profound. As we venture into these new territories, it is essential to consider how this knowledge can be used ethically and inclusively. The possibility of manipulating or reading thoughts raises issues of mental privacy and autonomy that require careful and thoughtful regulation. At the same time, equitable access to quantum technologies and practices is fundamental to preventing new forms of inequality and ensuring that benefits are distributed fairly.

Looking to the future, the research prospects on the connections between the mind and quantum physics promise to open new frontiers. Developments in quantum computers, brain-computer interfaces, and quantum medicine could revolutionize various fields, from health to education, from science to artificial intelligence. These innovations could not only improve the quality of life but also radically change our understanding of ourselves and the world.

The journey through the quantum mind has also led us to reflect on broader concepts such as the nature of free will, the interconnectedness of all things, and the role of intention in creating reality. These reflections invite us to reconsider our worldview and develop a greater awareness of our potential and responsibilities. In a universe where mind and matter are deeply interconnected, every thought, emotion, and action has significance and impact.

In conclusion, the journey through the quantum mind is a vast exploration that challenges our beliefs and opens new possibilities. This field of study offers us powerful tools to enhance our daily lives, stimulates deep reflections on the ethical and social implications of scientific discoveries, and pushes us toward a future rich in potential and innovation. As we continue to explore these invisible connections, we can expect to discover new wonders that will enrich our understanding of the mind and reality, leading us to live more consciously, intentionally, and harmoniously.

If you think you enjoyed this book

and it helped you, I kindly ask you to take just a few

seconds to leave a brief review on Amazon!

Thank you,

Marco Silvestri

Printed in Great Britain
by Amazon